Award-winning writer, television broadcaster and author of numerous bestsellers, **Leslie Kenton** is described by the press as the 'guru of health and fitness' and 'the most original voice in health'. A shining example of energy and commitment, she is highly respected for her thorough reporting. Leslie was born in California, and is the daughter of jazz musician Stan Kenton. After leaving Stanford University she journeyed to Europe in her early twenties, settling first in Paris, then in Britain where she has since remained. She has raised four children on her own by working as a television broadcaster, novelist, writer and teacher on health and for fourteen years was health and beauty editor at *Harpers & Queen*.

Leslie's writing on mainstream health is internationally known and has appeared in *Vogue*, the *Sunday Times*, *Cosmopolitan*, and the *Daily Mail*. She is the author of many other health books including: *The New Raw Energy* – co-authored with her daughter Susannah – *The New Biogenic Diet, The New Joy of Beauty, The New Ageless Ageing, Cellulite Revolution, 10 Day Clean-Up Plan, Endless Energy, Nature's Child, Lean Revolution, 10 Day De-Stress Plan* and *Passage to Power*. She turned to fiction with *Ludwig* – her first novel. Former consultant to a medical corporation in the USA and to the Open University's Centre of Continuing Education, Leslie's writing has won several awards including the PPA 'Technical Writer of the Year'. Her work was honoured by her being asked to deliver the McCarrison Lecture at the Royal Society of Medicine. In recent years she has become increasingly concerned not only with the process of enhancing individual health but also with re-establishing bonds with the earth as a part of helping to heal the planet.

Also by Leslie Kenton

THE JOY OF BEAUTY
ULTRAHEALTH
RAW ENERGY (with Susannah Kenton)
RAW ENERGY RECIPES (with Susannah Kenton)
AGELESS AGEING
THE BIOGENIC DIET
10 DAY CLEAN-UP PLAN
CELLULITE REVOLUTION
ENDLESS ENERGY (with Susannah Kenton)
NATURE'S CHILD
LEAN REVOLUTION
10 DAY DE-STRESS PLAN
THE NEW JOY OF BEAUTY
THE NEW ULTRAHEALTH
THE NEW AGELESS AGEING
THE NEW BIOGENIC DIET
THE NEW RAW ENERGY (with Susannah Kenton)
PASSAGE TO POWER
RAW ENERGY FOOD COMBINING DIET
JUICE HIGH (with Russell Cronin)
TEN STEPS TO ENERGY
REJUVENATE NOW
THE RAW ENERGY BIBLE
TEN STEPS TO A NEW YOU
TEN STEPS TO A NATURAL MENOPAUSE

QUICK FIX SERIES
Boost Energy
Look Great
Sleep Deep
Get Fit
Lose Fat
Beat Stress
Juice Blitz
Detox Now
Chill Out
Kick Colds

Fiction
LUDWIG (a spiritual thriller)

Ten Steps
to a **Younger You**

Leslie Kenton

Vermilion
London

1 3 5 7 9 10 8 6 4 2

Text copyright © Leslie Kenton 2000

The right of Leslie Kenton to be identified as the author
of this book has been asserted by her in accordance
with the Copyright, Designs and Patents Act, 1988.

First published in the United Kingdom in 1996 by Vermilion
as *Rejuvenate Now*

This new edition published in 2000 by Vermilion
an imprint of Ebury Press
Random House
20 Vauxhall Bridge Road
London SW1V 2SA

Random House Australia (Pty) Limited
20 Alfred Street, Milsons Point, Sydney,
New South Wales 2061, Australia

Random House New Zealand Limited
18 Poland Road, Glenfield,
Auckland 10, New Zealand

Random House (Pty) Limited
Endulini, 5A Jubilee Road,
Parktown 2193, South Africa

Random House Canada
1265 Aerowood Drive, Mississauga
Ontario L4W 1B9, Canada

Random House UK Limited Reg. No. 954009

A CIP catalogue record for this book is available from the British Library

ISBN: 0 09 182597 0

Printed and bound by Cox & Wyman Ltd, Reading, Berkshire

Contents

Foreword

This book explores the life-enhancing properties of diet and natural technologies for rejuvenating mind and body. It offers information about how diet, nutrition, movement and hydrotherapy together with simple mental techniques can be used to help strengthen the immune system, expand awareness, de-age the body and reverse degeneration.

Light nutrient-rich/calorie-poor eating, including a good portion of raw foods, enhances life energy. It is through the enhancement of life energy that natural age reversal takes place. Such energy cannot be quantified in chemical terms alone. Yet working with it can bring about age reversal as measured by orthodox medical parameters such as lowered cholesterol and blood pressure, improved insulin resistance and the loss of many symptoms normally associated with ageing. It can also help enhance our mental clarity, improve our emotional balance and heighten vitality.

Here is a simple-to-follow 10-day programme based on diet and natural rejuvenation techniques. It also points the way towards an ongoing lifestyle to help you continue the de-ageing process.

The information it contains is in no way intended to be prescriptive, to replace medical advice, or be a substitute for a good doctor or well-trained health-care practitioner – preferably one knowledgeable in nutrition and natural healing. If you are ill or suspect you are ill it is important that you see a physician. If you have been taking prescription medication, don't change your diet or use any of the natural rejuvenation technologies described here without consulting your doctor. Neither the publisher nor the author can accept responsibility for injuries or illness arising out of a failure by a reader to take medical advice.

I want to make clear that I have no commercial interest in any product, treatment or organization mentioned in this book. I do however have a profound interest in helping myself and others to maximize their potential for positive health, awareness and creativity. For it is my belief that the more each one of us is able to re-establish harmony within ourselves and with our environment, the better equipped we will be to wrestle with the challenges now facing our planet.

Leslie Kenton
Pembrokeshire, 2000

THE PRINCIPLES

Step 1
In the Zone

Athletes have a great phrase: *in the zone*. They use it to describe an almost perfect state of maximum mental, physical, and psychological performance – a sense of total wellbeing. Children experience it. Yet as we get older we tend to lose it. *Ten Steps to a Younger You* is designed to help you regenerate your energy, rejuvenate your body and rediscover the joys of living 'in the zone'. Your body and mind are relaxed. You feel centred, focused and dynamic. Your skin is smooth and glowing, your muscles are firm and strong, your movements are fluid, your eyes shine, and when you awaken in the morning you feel excitement about the day ahead as a child does.

Looking good and feeling great have nothing to do with how old you are as measured in years. They reflect a metabolic state in which your system is balanced and working at peak efficiency. This can happen at any age and is the goal of rejuvenation. Rejuvenation is a very real phenomenon. It can not only be experienced subjectively as you watch it happening to you, it can also be measured objectively in black-and-white clinical terms.

De-Ageing Starts Here

Ageing experts worldwide agree on certain *biomarkers* of ageing. These are simple tests used to establish a person's *biological* rather than *chronological* age. They range from measurements of vital capacity (how much air you can expel in a certain time), visual acuity and reaction time to fasting glucose levels, blood cholesterol, blood pressure, skin elasticity, and hormone levels. As your body becomes rejuvenated such measurements return to more youthful levels. Once this happens it is far less likely that you will fall prey to small illnesses like colds, 'flu, and allergic reactions. If you do become ill it is always a milder illness. When it comes to chronic illnesses such as cancer, heart disease, arthritis, diabetes and other degenerative con-ditions, living in the zone keeps you highly protected from them all, as it does from premature ageing. Every ageing expert worth his salt will tell you, by the way, that most of what we call ageing is premature and avoidable.

The aim of *The 10-Day Plan* is simple. It is to use well researched, clinically tested natural means to activate the powers of nature from within. This is an intensive programme to nourish body and soul by flooding your system with healing factors and subtle energies drawn from natural foods, natural movement, stimulation from hot and cold water, and transformative anti-stress mind tools. Used together they can set you on the road to clearing away both mental and physical rubbish which interferes with normal metabolism, suppresses natural vitality, and impedes the full expression of who you are. This is the first major step in rejuvenating body, mind and spirit. *Ten Steps to a Younger You* then offers guidelines to help you create an ongoing natural lifestyle for yourself to continue the process of de-ageing year after year.

Nature's Technologies

Why natural? Because natural techniques work best. For generations the principles of natural healing have been used successfully throughout the world. Until recently their efficacy had largely to be taken on faith. Now study after study – from Dr Dean Ornish's work on reversing coronary heart disease to Dr Roy Walford's experiments in longevity – confirms that natural approaches work best to reverse degenerative conditions, even where drug-based medicine fails. Little wonder, since our bodies have been genetically programmed to respond to food and water, movement and mind games, throughout the million years of our evolution. The techniques we will be working with are also inexpensive and easy to carry out at home for yourself. Here are a few of their benefits.

THE PAYOFFS

- **A Younger Body:** Functional not chronological age is what matters. Rejuvenating the body means lower blood pressure, cholesterol, fasting blood sugar and white blood cell count as well as improved resistance to disease and increased vitality.

- **Better Eyesight:** In middle age most people find the lens of the eye thickens and hardens which makes it difficult to see at all distances. This is the 'hold the newspaper two feet away to read it' syndrome. Begun before this happens, this kind of natural de-ageing programme can delay and even prevent this from happening. Begun after its appearance, it can slow down the degenerative process and often improve vision.

● **Smoother Skin:** The look of your skin – the largest organ in the body – tells a lot about the state of your body. As the body detoxifies and metabolic processes are rebuilt, skin that has lost its tone, become wrinkled and grown puffy becomes younger-looking. Nutrient-rich/calorie-poor eating coupled with hydrotherapy also offers the best possible anti-oxidant protection you can get against wrinkles, sags and ageing skin.

● **Energy To Spare:** A phenomenal increase in energy comes from nutrient-rich light eating which enables the body to clear itself of a significant amount of stored wastes. This is nothing more than the emergence of natural vitality which has become suppressed by over-feeding on nutritionally-depleted foods or by a lifestyle that did not encourage high-level health.

● **Emotional Balance and Mental Clarity:** A diet free of junk foods and excess fats helps release you from the sort of metabolic disturbance which causes mood swings and depression. Coupled with the natural technologies that make up *Ten Steps to a Younger You* it will help enhance your emotional balance and mental clarity.

Nature Goes Mainstream

Once, the natural techniques that form the core of *Ten Steps to a Younger You* were only used by doctors and health care practitioners trained in alternatives to conventional medicine to help restore integrity – mentally, physically and spiritually. Now, many have gone mainstream. Scientific research and clinical practice has begun to validate what experts in natural healing have been saying for generations, and the bridge between orthodox and natural healing is being more firmly built with each year that passes. So much so that many of the natural methods for prevention of premature ageing and degenerative diseases now form the most revolutionary and exciting field of medical research today.

A diet which is *nutrient-rich* yet *calorie-poor* has been shown to be the simplest and most effective way to heighten immunity, reverse degenerative conditions and produce a high level of wellbeing at any age. Highly orthodox organizations such as the American National Cancer Institute now actively pursue studies in the realm of nutrition involving micro-nutrients, phyto-chemicals (i.e. plant-based), enzymes, fibre, fat and vitamins. Meanwhile, virtually all health care professionals, from doctors to naturopaths – even the most dyed-in-the-wool conservatives – now admit that 70% of all cancers and other degenerative conditions are related in a significant way to how we eat and live.

Healthy from Within

Ten Steps to a Younger You is designed to help you change for the better as easily and quickly as possible. It presents a way of eating and living that draws on the very latest research findings about how lifestyle changes can improve the integrity of the immune system, and how nutrient-rich caloric limitation prolongs youth and life. Rejuvenating the body, regenerating energy and then living year after year 'in the zone' requires you to develop such a lifestyle – one that supports your needs physically, emotionally and spiritually in the best possible way. This means learning new skills and maybe also letting go of outdated behaviour patterns.

Based upon the tried and tested principles of detoxification and rebuilding, *The 10-Day Plan* works simultaneously to clear away the old and to build a new path to youthful living. The simple techniques that form its cornerstones can help us cast our habits, introduce us to new levels of aliveness, and bring us closer and closer to living 'in the zone'. Here they are.

THE 10-DAY PLAN

Cornerstones

One: Clean Sweep Diet

Every calorie you eat during Clean Sweep comes from a highly nutritional source to help detoxify the body and help rebuild metabolism both biochemically and energetically. The diet is low in fat and salt, high in fresh raw vegetables and full of natural unprocessed foods. It supplies your cells with easily assimilated nutrients to strengthen their natural defences. It also uses foods which contain huge quantities of naturally-occuring phytochemicals which science has discovered to be the real powerhouses for preventing and reversing degeneration.

Two: Psychic Scrub

We all carry around false ideas, notions and habit patterns making us highly susceptible to early ageing. Psychic rubbish, like physical rubbish, is a big energy-drainer. It can cause as much free radical damage and as many distortions in life energy as can living on junk food or taking drugs. Rejuvenating the body and reclaiming life energy that has been locked up in unproductive thought patterns demands that we clear away the psychic junk, in exactly the way that Clean Sweep Diet clears the stored wastes from the body. That is where *autogenics* comes in – a tried and tested daily practice which can help clear away psychological blocks and lift off stress that has been suppressing vitality and creativity.

Three: Hydro-Electrics

Hydrotherapy is the oldest system of natural healing in the world. The Plan makes full use of the body's physiological responses to water as a powerful de-ageing tool. Water used externally in the form of hot and cold baths or showers stimulates the body to increase energy, balance hormones, tone muscles, and improve nervous system functioning and circulation. Water used internally helps you dissolve, transport and absorb nutrients as well as clear stored wastes. Hydrotherapy is a simple yet transformative tool for releasing static and stagnant physical and mental states and rebuilding high-level health and more youthful functioning.

Four: Reinventing the Body

Specially created rejuvenating processes based on the *Feldenkrais* system of movement, form the fourth cornerstone of *The 10-Day Plan*. They too are designed to help dissolve away restrictions. They can, in effect, 'reinvent' the body using *blissful* movements to alter our neurological patterning, clear physical discomforts and at the same time expand our capacity for joy.

Minus Nutrition

Clean Sweep Diet – *The 10-Day Plan's* first cornerstone – also addresses the issue of what the Japanese doctor Mitsuo Koda, one of the world's greatest living experts in natural healing, calls *minus nutrition*.

By this Koda means a way of eating that focuses not only on what you put *into* your body but also on how well you *eliminate* wastes and toxins. As yet in the West we give little thought to minus nutrition. We tend to concentrate on *plus* nutrition – the intake of proteins, fatty acids, fibre and nutrients. In fact, just about every conventional nutritional study carried out in Europe and America still focuses on plus nutrition. Yet plus nutrition is only half of the equation. Optimal health depends not only on what you take in, assimilate and metabolize but also on your ability swiftly and successfully to excrete waste matter so it doesn't accumulate. Without minus nutrition high level health is simply not possible. As in everything in nature, the taking in and giving out must be balanced. Clean Sweep shows you how to do this.

Trust Your Body

The natural technologies which form the foundation of *Ten Steps to a Younger You* are well tried and tested. Used daily with perseverance they are able to work wonders. Yet, good as they are, these techniques are only catalysts for change. It is the life force within us – not only the physical and chemical processes in the body, but also the mental and energetic fields that surround and permeate us – which do the work. The natural technologies only help us tap into our own organic control systems for balance, healing and regeneration.

We often forget how magnificent the body's innate control and regenerative mechanisms are. They continually maintain the body's temperature within a few tenths of a degree without a collection of thermometers or computers to check things out. The *pH* of our blood stays within a very narrow balance between acidity and alkalinity without our ever giving it a thought. When we cut a finger our body heals the cut. Seldom do we give much thought to the intricate processes by which all this occurs, nor do we stop to ponder on the breadth and depth of subliminal intelligence in each human being that directs our lives and oversees our health.

It is in the living body where the real magic lies – magic that can bring you smoother skin, more energy, a leaner, firmer body, better hormone balance, and greater stamina as well as better emotional balance and a new sense of freedom to 'be who you are' with ease.

Such are the promises of natural de-ageing which help add life to years as well as years to life. *Ten Steps to a Younger You* can not only introduce you to life 'in the zone' years from now, it could even help you to *die young late in life*.

Step 2
Rejuvenation Works

On February 6th 1996 the oldest woman in the world at that time celebrated her 121st birthday. Madame Jeanne Calment was born in France in 1875. In Britain there are now 2,370 people over 100 years old, and 2,100 of these are women. In the United States a million baby-boomers are now expected to reach their 100th birthday. By the first quarter of the next millennium 1 in 5 of the population in developed countries will be over 65 years of age. The over-nineties are the fastest growing age-group in the Western world.

Each decade more people live longer. If we are to alleviate the enormous cost to society in economic and human terms for an ageing population riddled with degenerative diseases, it is time we began making use of the latest findings about rejuvenation and putting them into practice in our own lives.

120 Years Young

Growing older does not have to be riddled with physical suffering and emotional alienation. It can actually mean growing *better*. Scientists studying the characteristics of the long-lived tell us we have a potential life-span of between 100 and 120 years – provided, that is, that we don't die from one of the degenerative conditions like stroke, heart disease, diabetes or cancer. So far, only a few of us are living out our potential.

Degenerative diseases which undermine our quality of life do not arrive as a twist of fate. They are largely the result of lifestyle: how we eat and exercise, how well or poorly we manage stress and how good we are at protecting ourselves from chemical pollution and from radiation in our environment.

As we approach the millennium rejuvenation is no longer a matter of wishful thinking. Experiments in natural healing and regeneration show that the degenerative changes previously associated with getting older are not, as they have been assumed to be, natural consequences of ageing, but rather the result of a lifestyle that does not support human health at its highest potential. Change your lifestyle for the better and you can rejuvenate your body. It is also likely that you will live longer. On the other hand, feast on highly processed convenience foods riddled with sugar, junk fats and chemical additives, forget to exercise regularly, manage stress poorly, use unnecessary drugs and expose yourself without protection to pollutants in air and water, and not only are you likely to age rapidly, you will also sow seeds for degenerative disease, from cancer and diabetes to arthritis, mental disorders, and heart troubles.

Human Promises

Inhabitants of the Japanese island of Okinawa eat a nutrient-rich diet containing 17–40% fewer calories than that of their brothers and sisters in the rest of Japan. Okinawans also experience only 59% as much heart disease, 59% stroke and 60% cancer as the rest of the Japanese. Okinawa also boasts at least five times as many centenarians as in the longest-living populations elsewhere in Japan.

Scientists who have studied other long-lived peoples of the world such as the Hunzas in Northern Kashmir, the Georgians in Russia, and the Vilcabamba Indians in South America, report that all of these peoples live on a nutrient-rich/calorie-poor diet high in fresh, uncooked foods. Like the Okinawans, they experience very few of the degenerative patterns that we do in the West.

In the 1960s scientists in Spain carried out an interesting rejuvenation experiment on two groups of elderly people living in a nursing home. They fed one group their normal diet, while the other group were fed a calorie-restricted diet rich in essential macro- and micro-nutrients. After three years of study, the scientists were able to confirm that those living on the nutrient-rich/calorie-poor diet had only half the rate of illnesses and half the rate of death of those who had been left free to eat whatever they wanted.

Youth Returns

Rejuvenation has finally moved out of the realm of monkey glands and Dorian Gray dreams. It is happening right now, from the shores of the American Pacific, through Europe, and on to Japan. And it is available now to those of us who are willing to put energy into accomplishing it. Rejuvenating ourselves is not only important in terms of personal payoffs such as enhanced vitality, good looks and radiant health, it can also help lift an enormous financial burden from society by reversing many degenerative conditions which cost the world dearly both economically and in terms of human suffering.

Thanks to cutting-edge research from scientists like Dr Dean Ornish at The Preventative Medical Research Institute in California and Dr Roy Walford of Biosphere II fame we now know that comprehensive lifestyle changes including improved diet, stress management and regular exercise, when made by people with degenerative conditions like coronary heart disease, will significantly regenerate the body. After a year on a programme such as Ornish's (which shuns convenience foods and uses a meat-, fish- and poultry-free vegetarian diet of fruits, vegetables, whole grains, legumes and soya products) over 80% of the people taking part experienced a regression in arterial fatty deposits, as well as a reversal of most of the other accepted biomarkers of ageing. So seriously is the research of Ornish now taken by those who hold the medical purse-strings in the United States that his programme has become the first non-surgical, non-pharmaceutical therapy for heart disease to qualify for tough American insurance reimbursements – something that has never happened before in the history of Western medicine.

Rejuvenating Rats

The work of Dr Roy Walford is world renowned in the field of age retardation. Professor at the University of California at Los Angeles School of Medicine, Walford and his colleagues spent many years studying the effect of nutrient-rich/calorie-poor diets on animals. They wanted to expand the work of Clive McKay, first carried out in 1935. McKay discovered that rats fed a calorie-restricted diet lived twice as long as rats fed an ordinary diet. Walford and his colleagues were not only able to replicate McKay's findings, they were able to take them much further, even exploring the implications of dietary change on humans.

Experiments on animals using dietary restriction have been going on for sixty years with enormous success. Science has shown that simply by cutting the calories in an animal's diet early on in its life, and by making sure that the fodder they eat is high in essential macro- and micro-nutrients, animal lifespan is significantly extended. When this kind of dietary change is initiated in mid-life the animal goes through a natural process of rejuvenation: its fur becomes more beautiful, if it is fat it sheds weight, and its organism returns to a more youthful way of functioning, both biochemically and physiologically. This same healing process takes place in everything from single-cell pond animals to mammals such as mice and rats. Researchers have established that the bodies of animals can be rejuvenated in real, scientifically measurable ways through dietary change. So can our own bodies. And it is never too late to begin.

Enter Biosphere II

The most recent and exciting human research into the effect of a calorie-restricted, nutrient-rich diet has been carried out by Roy Walford. Walford himself has lived on a nutrient-rich/calorie-poor diet for many years. Recently he and seven of his colleagues sealed themselves inside a closed environment for two years – Biosphere II – in the Arizona desert, which was intended to duplicate the earth's environment. There, these eight participants raised nutritious foods. Their daily fare consisted mostly of vegetables, fruits and grains plus a small quantity of goat's milk and yoghurt and a once-a-week serving of meat or fish and one egg. The average calorie intake during their first six months was 1,800 calories a day. It then rose for the remaining 18 months to 2,200 a day. To their surprise the people taking part did not feel particularly hungry. This nutrient-rich, bulky, calorie-poor way of eating fills your stomach and satisfies your hunger. In fact, if you happen to be a persistent crash dieter you can find eating as much food as you need on this kind of diet a bit of a challenge.

The rejuvenation these people experienced was remarkable. All of them, regardless of age or sex, registered changes in blood pressure, cholesterol, and triglycerides, paralleling the rejuvenating changes witnessed in animal studies. During the first six months the men had an average weight loss of 18%, their body fat stabilizing at between 6–10%. The women experienced a weight loss of 10%, with body fat stabilizing at 10–15%. Fasting blood sugar levels also dropped on average 20%, cholesterol levels by 38% and blood pressure by 30% – and then stabilized at more youthful levels. As Walford says in his fascinating book *The Anti-Ageing Plan*, 'no other long-term sustainable diet has ever been shown to produce changes as dramatic as these . . . You will live longer, you will need less sleep, you'll have a sharper mind, you'll feel better, you'll get fewer colds, 'flu, and be generally less susceptible to other diseases.'

Oriental Secrets

Since 1983 the eating habits of over 6,500 mainland Chinese have been exhaustively studied, while another 10,500 Chinese from the mainland and Taiwan have been surveyed by researchers as part of the massive and ongoing China-Cornell-Oxford Diet and Health Project. The project is led by nutritional biochemist Dr T Colin Campbell from Cornell University and Dr Chen Junshi of the Chinese Institute of Nutrition and Food Hygiene in Beijing. Some fascinating information has already come out of their investigations. The Chinese consume only 6–24% of their calories in fat, while we in the West take in 35–45% of our calories from fat sources. They don't eat sweets the way we do at the end of a meal. They don't eat convenience foods either. They *do* eat lots of sea vegetables, grains, green vegetables such as kale, mustard greens, amaranth and long-leafed water spinach. They also eat many foods based on the soya bean such as tempeh (slabs of cultured soybeans), tofu, yuba (thin elastic sheets lifted off the top of hot soya milk), and miso (a fermented soybean paste) and tamari or soy sauce.

Sea vegetables are important for health. They help supply the body with an excellent balance of minerals and trace elements which convenience foods and chemically fertilized foods lack. The green foods are important too – both for their high level of easily assimilated vitamins and minerals and because they are rich in all sorts of plant-based anti-oxidants, some of which are far more potent than vitamins in protecting the body from free radical damage, as well as other biologically active phyto-chemicals. These phyto-chemicals include the *indoles* found in Brussels sprouts and dark green leafy vegetables, and *sulforaphane* found in broccoli and kale. These substances help fight cancer, and age-inhibiting enzymes help remove toxic wastes from the cells.

The soya-based foods so beloved of Oriental peoples play an important part in rejuvenating the body. They are replete in phyto-hormones – weak plant-based hormones such as *genistein,* an *isoflavone* which is now believed to help protect against cancer, heart disease, osteoporosis, and menopausal and menstrual symptoms in women. These gentle plant-based oestrogens also help protect the bodies of men and women from the devastating consequences of our being continually exposed to the powerful and dangerous petro-chemically derived *xenoestrogens* or 'oestrogen mimics' in our environment. Xenoestrogens are present in pesticides, herbicides and plastics, and they continue to disrupt reproductive processes in people and animals. They are believed to be responsible for the huge drop reported in sperm count –

almost fifty per cent in the last fifty years in the Western world – as well as for disruption in the balance of reproductive hormones in women's bodies that has contributed greatly to the rising incidence of PMS, infertility, endometriosis, fibroids, menopausal miseries and osteoporosis in recent years.

Let's Get It Together

Meanwhile, in another corner of the Orient, tucked away amidst the endless twisting and turning streets of Osaka in Japan, is Mitsuo Koda's remarkable clinic. There people from all over the world come to learn the art of self-cure and rejuvenation under Dr Koda's guidance. Born in 1924, Koda graduated from Osaka University Medical School. Like almost every great medical innovator who has worked in natural health – Max Bircher-Benner in Switzerland, Max Gerson in Germany, and Francis Pottenger in the United States, for instance – Koda came to his understanding of healing by having to wrestle with his own serious illness after finding that orthodox medicine could do nothing to help him. He began to study natural technologies for healing and to test them out, first on himself and then on others, with excellent results. Since then, for over forty years, this lean and vital doctor has fed over six thousand people a nutrient-rich/calorie-poor diet and used other simple natural techniques, obtaining phenomenal results.

Koda's successes, wrought through changes in diet, simple exercises, hydrotherapy and prayer, have been witnessed in patients who come through his clinic with a wide variety of illnesses, from atopic eczema and collagen diseases to cancer, vascular disease, diabetes and AIDS. One can state unequivocally that what Koda calls *light eating* both rejuvenates the body and delays ageing. His clinical experiences are confirmed by Japanese doctors and scientists who have examined the results of his treatments, all of which are based on long-standing natural technologies.

Over the course of many years, Koda discovered for himself two important things. Firstly, he found that the methods of *naturecure*, the aim of which is to help the body heal itself from within, are based upon the same principles throughout the world, and vary little in practice. Secondly, he found that what many great nature doctors had taught before him is true: the fundamental cause of degeneration and most chronic illness is toxicity or uneliminated waste – *shukuben* in Japanese.

Shukuben Ages

The concept of *shukuben* – stagnated faeces in the colon leading to uneliminated waste in the rest of the body – can be hard for the average doctor to grasp, for our Western doctors are trained in interventionist medicine and drug treatment. They tend to accept the notion that illness is either visited upon the body as an accident of fate (as in the case of cancer or rheumatoid arthritis) or as a direct result of exposure to some kind of micro-organism (as in colds or 'flu). The tradition of natural medicine to which Koda's work belongs, however, has long insisted that premature ageing, degenerative illness and infectious diseases will not take seed in a body unburdened with toxicity. The first task therefore in rejuvenating and healing the person is to eliminate toxicity that has been stored in the body. In no small part this is a question of redefining our eating-habits and re-educating ourselves in our approach to what we eat.

Eat Light

Koda reduces the food intake of his patients and students to about 60% of normal calorie intake. To do this he makes use of a very high level of raw foods and green foods. From a biochemical point of view, shukuben causes free radical damage, and free radical damage is right at the core of premature ageing and degeneration. A high-raw diet detoxifies the body, eliminates the accumulation of shukuben in the colon which most of us carry around for decades, (despite the fact that we may be having 'normal' bowel movements every day), and quells free radical damage. Meanwhile green foods replenish heath-enhancing vitamins, minerals and plant factors to rebuild a person's vitality and help restore biochemical balance. The nutrient-rich/calorie-poor, high green, light eating which Koda recommends also helps guard the body from accumulating further toxic wastes. 'Once the accumulation of shukuben is halted', says Koda, 'the body is highly protected against premature degeneration and disease, both acute and chronic.'

By the way, Koda's light eating, like Walford's nutrient-rich/calorie-poor fare, have absolutely nothing to do with going on a slimming regime – far from it. In creating a nutrient-rich/calorie-poor diet, you have to be extremely choosy about the quality of food that you eat. And, while modern nutritionists consider a diet of 3,000 calories or more to be necessary to maintain health in an adult person, the experience of age researchers shows quite clearly that this is not the case. In the thousands of recorded clinical cases at Dr Koda's clinic, healthy people have been shown to be able to carry out normal daily activities on between 1,000–1,800 calories a day – sometimes even less.

Quantum Foods

Raw vegetables, whole grains, and the super green foods are *quantum foods* – the very best. These days it is virtually impossible to get all of the essential elements of nutrition needed for successful light eating without using them. They contain nutritional elements not found to the same degree or quality in other foods. Vitamins, minerals and trace elements as well as proteins and fatty acids are found in raw vegetables in a quantity and balance that is *qualitatively* different to that in the same foods when they are heated or processed. As Koda says: '25 grammes of protein from raw food is equivalent to 75 grammes of protein from cooked food.' When five to ten types of different raw vegetables – including root vegetables such as carrots, radishes and parsnips, and leaf vegetables like spinach, cabbage, and kohlrabi – are eaten each day in their fresh state as salads, in soups, and as green drinks, other nutritional supplements are often unnecessary.

Assistant professor Dr T Hazama at Osaka City University carried out some interesting studies on active people eating an all-raw vegetable diet which consists of raw green vegetable juice made from spinach, cabbage, lettuce, celery, and other greens, raw brown rice powder, Japanese grated radish, grated carrot and grated yam. He discovered that the performance of athletes improved significantly despite the fact that their base metabolic rate decreased by around 40%. Such findings contradict the generally accepted notion that an athlete needs vast extra quantities of calories and protein because of the activity that he or she is involved in, as well as the notion that for high performance a high metabolic rate is necessary. Age researchers frequently report that nutrient-rich/calorie-poor eating tends to lower metabolism. Yet, rather than being a negative thing, many believe this is a major reason why it may help prolong life.

Live Long and Prosper

I personally interviewed a great many of Koda's ex-patients. These were men and women of all ages who, after experiencing remission of their various conditions, continued to live on this light diet. They were all extremely vital. Some were fully capable of running marathons (and did!) despite the fact that many had been living on a diet lower in calories than that which traditional, orthodox nutrition insists is healthy.

Much work still needs to be done in order to understand from a scientific point of view just *how* Koda's nutrient-rich light eating makes this possible. How, for instance, can the body thrive on the relatively low levels of protein? Some scientists believe that, when presented with the highest quality of fresh raw vegetables and grains, the body may even be capable of recycling its old nitrogen – the element necessary for the formation of new protein. Dr T Okuda, Assistant Professor in the Department of Nutritional Science of Osaka City University, discovered that on the Koda diet a person eating 1,000 calories does not excrete urea in the urine. This is highly unusual since the elimination of urea from someone on a so-called normal diet is approximately 30 grammes a day. A few researchers now speculate that the reason urea is not excreted in the urine of people on the Koda diet is that the 'friendly' bacteria in the intestines and colon may actually be re-assimilating the urea and using its nitrogen to build more protein. Whatever the reasons – and there are probably many – something remarkable is certainly going on.

Benevolence Towards All

Koda loves to quote an old Japanese saying which translates roughly as, 'Eat light to maintain your might.' As he also points out, 'food is life'. Food is not merely a *thing*, as many people assume. Human beings, he insists, like all living creatures, receive life from the 'life' of food. Eating light is, to this extent, killing as little life as possible. As Koda says, 'It is a concrete demonstration of love and benevolence to the life on this planet.'

The work of such people as Ornish, Walford, Campbell, Chen Junshi and Koda, like that of the other great pioneers in natural health and healing, holds tremendous promise for those of us who want to explore the potential of regeneration and rejuvenation to a degree that until now has only been dreamed of – regardless of how old we are right now.

Step 3
Free Rads & Rockers

The secrets of ageing are hidden deep within the molecular structure of the living organism. One of the great biological mysteries, ageing is a universal phenomenon – a simple fact of being alive. But how rapidly it occurs is by no means universal. By now much research has been carried out into the processes of ageing and all sorts of theories have developed about how and why it happens. One, the *ageing clock* theory, sees ageing as programmed by a preset number of cell divisions, the time between which is said to determine our lifespan. Another, *the cross-linking of protein* theory, suggests that molecular alterations in the body's protein molecules cause microfibres to be laid down creating loss of elasticity, stiffness and degeneration. A third, the *errors in DNA* theory insists that chemical exposure, general toxicity and basic genetic tendencies distort the DNA, or genetic material, of cells so they can no longer reproduce normally. Still other theories claim ageing comes from *changes in brain function* to undermine the function and regulation of balance in hormones and the nervous system, or from *autoimmunity* where the immune function declines, or from *stress*. The one thing that all theories of ageing seem to have in common is recognition that degeneration is associated with free radical damage. The more free radical damage takes place, the older you get. The more you are protected from free radical damage the more you are protected from ageing.

Free Rad Politics

Ten years ago the word 'free radical' sounded to most ears like a left-wing political activist. Not only did few know what free radicals were, the idea that free radical damage underlies both the ageing process and the development of degenerative diseases like heart disease, cancer, diabetes and arthritis seemed absurd. Nowadays we know different. Free radicals are all the rage. Every other book on health you come across is warning about the dangers of free radicals and telling you to take lots of vitamins A, C, and E to protect yourself from these horrible demons.

A free radical is a molecule with an unpaired electron, lustfully searching for a mate. There are several kinds of free radicals. Oxygen free radicals are particularly malevolent. They react quickly and greedily with other molecules. When they find a mate – and just about any mate will do – they can destroy cell membranes, disrupt DNA and wreak havoc with the body. Many things cause the production of free radicals. Air pollution, for instance, being exposed to ultra-violet light or radiation, pesticides in foods, drugs, cigarette smoke, exposure to some plastics, and even polyunsaturated fats. Flying in jets also produces free radicals, as does living at a high altitude, because in both cases you are subject to high levels of gamma radiation. Even exercise produces free radicals. And the experts on ageing are right: free radicals *do* cause terrible damage to the body – but only when they are produced in *excess*. There are lots of good things to be said about free radicals as well. This is something all those little books and articles on swallowing more ACE vitamins fail to tell you.

Energy Equations

What makes energy-yielding metabolism possible in our bodies – in effect what keeps us alive – is the ability that we have evolved throughout the ages to take nutrients in through our foods and convert them into chemical and bio-electrical energy. We do this through oxidation, or burning, in a process known as *aerobic metabolism*. Enzymes in the body – living catalysts – carefully control a series of small steps which liberate the maximum amount of energy present for effective use, while causing the minimum amount of disturbance to our cells. This enormously efficient way of producing and releasing energy involves the transfer of electrons from one molecule to another. Scientists call this transfer an *oxidation-reduction,* or a *redox reaction*. So long as we live redox reactions take place ceaselessly. The trouble is – and here's where free radical damage comes in – a number of highly reactive, potentially toxic and destructive species of molecules are generated in the process.

The greater the bodily activity at any particular place or time, the more free radicals we generate. Our brain is particularly demanding of energy. About 20% of our body's oxygen consumption is used by the brain. This gives the brain an enormous amount of energy but it also creates a fertile ground for free radicals to breed. Surges of various hormones in our bodies such as *adrenaline* and *noradrenaline* generate hydrogen peroxide, which can also result in the formation of more free radicals – so much so that we frequently generate more than our anti-oxidant defence mechanisms can handle. Most free radicals are generated during the day. Some researchers believe that free radical formation in the daytime and free radical quenching that occurs at night while we sleep may be the driving power behind the *circadian rhythms* – that is, the biological control of events in the body.

10,000 Hits A Day

What is amazing is just how extensive free radical activity is in the human body. One of the leading experts in free radical biochemistry, Dr Bruce Ames at the University of California at Berkeley, estimates that every cell in our body experiences 10,000 free radical 'hits' each day of our life. A well nourished, healthy body is equipped to handle them. We have inside our bodies amazing anti-oxidant defence mechanisms involving enzymes like *glutathione-peroxidase*, *super-oxide dismutase* and *catalase*. Provided we are leading a balanced life, eating plenty of fresh foods, getting optimum amounts of exercise, and are not exposed to excessive amounts of chemical pollution, all should go well.

What's happening to many of us, however, is that we are subjected to more free radical activity than our natural anti-oxidant mechanisms can detoxify. Then we get oxidation damage as excess free rads wreak havoc with our bodies. They can form cataracts in the eyes, trigger Alzheimer's disease, cause premature ageing and the build-up of cholesterol in the arteries, and provoke a thousand other negative changes associated with ageing. The latest research indicates that free radical damage to the cells' 'energy factories' – the mitochondria – gradually interferes with the production of ATPH, the body's energy currency, thus further increasing free radical output. This in turn impairs all functions so that tissues and organs become less able to cope with challenges and the body as a whole degenerates. Meanwhile, we feel older and look older and have less and less vitality.

Strange Paradox

So free radicals put us in the strange position of being totally dependent upon them for our life energy, yet completely susceptible to their toxic effects – what in biochemistry is know as *oxidizing-stress* or *oxy-stress*. It is this oxy-stress which poses a continuous challenge to the integrity of our cells and tissues. As the free radical enthusiasts point out, this is the central cause of premature ageing.

The key to making free radical biochemistry work *for* you instead of *against* you is balance. When there are too many free radicals produced in your system as a result of poor digestion, or stress, or exposure to excessive ultra-violet light, or pollutants in air and water, then you suffer oxy-stress. Anti-oxidants such as vitamins A, C, and E, beta carotene, Co Enzyme Q10, selenium and many potent plant-based factors like *pycogynol* help quench oxy-stress and prevent free radical damage. So nowadays we are continually urged to take more of these substances if we want to prevent premature ageing and illness. Yet this is not quite as simple as the free radical rockers would have us believe. And popping pills is not always the best way to go about it.

Gung Ho

Twenty years ago, having interviewed some of the world's top anti-ageing experts, I became aware of the importance of taking anti-oxidants to protect the body. Later, when I was writing *Ageless Ageing*, I put into practice what they taught me. To put it simply: the more anti-oxidants you take, the healthier and the better protected from premature ageing you will be.

Yet as the years passed, certain things began to bother me. I wanted to know, for instance, how much of the various anti-oxidants is *enough*? And can you take too many? I couldn't understand how free radicals could be so bad since they were also necessary for life. Finally I was curious about my own body's reaction to taking high doses of anti-oxidants – 1,600 iu vitamin E, 150,000 iu of mixed carotinoids and 10 grammes of vitamin C a day. Doing all this, I figured, should have had me feeling full of energy. Yet as the years passed I found myself more and more fatigued, despite being perfectly well. None of it made sense.

I figured if you want the straight story you had better get it from the horse's mouth. So I went back to the work done by Dr Denham Harmon, the man who way back in 1954 conceived the free radical theory of ageing – one of the most celebrated experts on ageing in the world.

Free Rad Facts and Fictions

Denham Harmon is an extraordinary researcher. Like most great scientists, what he writes is easy to understand, even to a non-technical person. He writes about free radicals very much as a philosopher might explore life and death – yet at a molecular level. Harmon's work makes it clear that free radical reactions are essential to life. Indeed it is likely to be redox reactions that produced life on earth and which largely engineered evolution through their effect on DNA. Harmon is also quite clear that for high level health and the prevention of premature ageing most of us need to use anti-oxidants in some form from the age of 27 onwards. And does he take anti-oxidants himself? You bet he does. Yet not in excess, as some anti-ageing enthusiasts urge us to do. He takes them in *moderate* doses – 400 iu vitamin E and 2 grammes vitamin C, 30 mg co-enzyme Q-10, plus 25,000 iu beta carotene every other day. He would take more, he says, but he *can't afford to be fatigued*.

Forget Magic Bullets

What does this mean when just about every book and article on ageing these days urges us to take more and more? It means that in all our enthusiasm to get on the free radical bandwagon many of us have fallen into the same trap of mechanistic thinking that limits much of orthodox medicine. In an attempt to slow ageing we tend to treat anti-oxidants as 'magic bullets', and to lose all awareness of the importance of inter-relationships between them and synergy in the body. More anti-oxidants does not necessarily mean better.

Taking too many anti-oxidant supplements can eventually leave you chronically tired with weak muscles. Harmon and his colleagues discovered through animal experiments that very large quantities of anti-oxidants such as *BHT* – a synthetic commonly used as a food preservative – will actually suppresses the proper functioning of the *mitochondria* (the little energy factories in the cells), as well as the production of *ATP* (the body's own energy currency). There is no question that we need anti-oxidants, yet there is no simple answer as to exactly how much of vitamin E, selenium, vitamin C, and the carotenoids we optimally take.

Go For Balance

I had been taking *too many* anti-oxidant supplements. Don't get me wrong. These free radical scavengers did work. I looked around me to find that my skin was not falling apart as was that of many friends of the same age, yet I still had this problem with energy. After learning what I should have known all along I cut down my intake of anti-oxidant nutrients only to find that within a couple of weeks my energy increased dramatically.

Recently The Alliance for Ageing Research, a non-profit organization based in Washington DC, recommended that people who are generally healthy need somewhere between 100–400 iu of vitamin E, 17,500–50,000 iu beta-carotene, and 200–1,000 mg of vitamin C a day. Exactly how much is right for *you* depends on a lot of things: Do you smoke? Do you live at high altitudes? Do you drink more than a glass of alcohol a day? Do you eat convenience foods rich in junk fats? Do you eat sugar? Doing any of these things increases your need for anti-oxidants. Eating a high-raw diet of fresh unprocessed foods dramatically decreases it.

Perfect Synergy

The most effective approach to de-ageing relies on getting anti-oxidants in the form in which they come in nature – by eating natural, unprocessed, fresh foods rich not only in the anti-oxidants that have been heavily studied and are well known, but in many other plant substances that in one way or anther have anti-ageing properties. One of the interesting things about the anti-ageing substances in fresh foods is that they also happen to be anti-cancer substances. The changes that take place in cancer are akin to the mutations to the cells, cell walls, and genetic material which occur as the body ages. Eat foods rich in anti-cancer compounds and you automatically protect your body from premature ageing too.

There are certain *superfoods* – herbs, mushrooms and

other plant substances – that are high on the list of powerful natural de-agers.They include the algae such as chlorella, spirulina, the Australian Dunaliella Salina; the seaweeds – dulse, kelp, alaria and bladderwrack; certain herbs with powerful *adaptogenic* properties that help protect the body from stress such as Fo-ti, Schizandra, astragalus, ginger and schizandra; cereal grasses, the immune-supporting Oriental mushrooms such as reishi and maitake, as well as natural plant anti-oxidants such as those found in sage, rosemary, and cloves. There are thousands of plant-based chemicals in natural foods, and some of them have even higher anti-oxidant activity than known anti-oxidant minerals and vitamins. Take grape seeds, for example. Within the seed of red grapes you will find very high levels of something called *procyanidolic oligomers* (PCOs), which contain some of the most active free radical scavengers known.

Enter Neutraceuticals

Neutraceuticals are the newest advances in dietary supplements. They are beginning to grace the shop shelves next to vitamin and mineral supplements. These new products contain phyto-chemical substances and compounds such as those from grape seeds which have been extracted from foods and then concentrated into powders and capsules. For example, now you can find that some of the cholesterol-lowering factors found in a clove of garlic and the cancer-preventing elements in a sprig of fresh raw broccoli have been put together into an easy-to-use form. These phyto-chemicals are always non-nutrient substances – that is, *not* vitamins, minerals, or trace elements. Some bring plants their colour, taste, and fragrance. Others enhance their natural defences against disease. In recent years scientists have discovered that many of these factors in plants can help protect us. The reason these new products are called neutraceuticals is because of their neutral action on the body. Unlike drugs they are very unlikely to cause side-effects. Yet some have been shown to slow tumour growth in cancer, others to combat hormone-related cancer risks, lower cholesterol levels and blood pressure, boost the immune system, prevent tooth decay and gum disease and help reverse many of the other biomarkers of ageing.

Researchers into the exciting new world of phyto-chemical biology have identified thousands of different plant chemicals that exist in natural foods, hundreds of which have already been shown to have health benefits. Here are a few of the most important recently discovered phyto-chemicals and some of their life-enhancing, anti-oxidant and anti-ageing actions:

ANTI-AGEING PHYTOCHEMICALS

Name	Where Found	Benefit
allicin	onions, garlic, leeks, spring onions	lowers LDL (the negative) blood cholesterol, detoxifies by enhancing production of glutathione S-transferase, helps protect against breast cancer and heart disease as well as colon cancer and stomach cancer, enhances immunity
alpha carotene	seaweeds and carrots	heightens immunity, slows growth of cancer cells in animals, may help prevent cardiovascular disease and inflammation
anthocyanins	cranberry juice	helps prevent and cure urinary tract infections
beta carotene	dark green vegetables, red & yellow vegetables such as carrot and marrow, peaches and apricots	decreases risk of many cancers including skin, colon, and female cancers. Also improves immune function

Name	Where Found	Benefit
catechins	green tea	together with polyphenol and theaflavin it lowers cholesterol, boosts fat metabolism and may boost immune functions as well as help prevent some cancers and much ageing
genistein	soy foods like tofu, soybeans, tamari, soya milk	may help protect against breast cancer, osteoporosis and other menstrual and menopausal disorders, and together with other phyto-chemicals contained in soya can help lower cholesterol and slow tumour growth in animals
indoles	cabbages, dark green vegetables	helps detoxify the body, protects against excessive oestrogen buildup, slows cancer growth in animals, enhances immune functions
limones	citrus fruits	protects against breast cancer in animals, heightens production of enzymes involved in detoxifying the body, helps lower blood cholesterol and reduce plaque in arteries
lycopene	red grapefruit, tomatoes, water-melon, apricots	protects against age-related cell damage and oxidation to proteins and fats
saponins	chickpeas, soybeans, lentils and other beans	help slow the rate of tumour growth in animals
sulforaphane	cauliflower, kale, turnip greens, Brussels sprouts	helps cancer-fighting and age-fighting enzymes detoxify cells, inhibits the development of breast cancer in animals
triterpenoids & glycyrrhizin	licorice root	enhances immune functions, has anti-tumour properties, fights gum disease and tooth decay, improves liver function by enhancing liver enzymes that help protect against excess oestrogens

Whole Foods Matter Most

The advantages of getting anti-oxidants naturally, in natural form, are many. When it comes to protecting the body nothing works like nature. Only nature herself creates the magnificent synergy of substances and compounds to which the body has become genetically programmed throughout evolution. Phyto-chemicals have an important part to play in rejuvenating the body and continuing to de-age it afterwards. This is why the Clean Sweep diet relies on foods rich in them and why the best nutritional supplements for de-ageing are phyto-chemically based. What comes first, however, and what is most important of all, always, is how you eat. A diet for de-ageing the body needs to be high-raw and rich in green vegetables, whole grains, fruits, beans and seeds. When you eat this way you get the very best complement of vitamins, minerals, phyto-chemicals and enzymes for free radical protection. And when it comes to de-ageing the body, enzymes move centre stage.

Step 4
Life In
Life Out

There is a well-known saying about computers: 'garbage in, garbage out'. The same can be said of the human body. Feed it on highly processed convenience foods grown on chemically-treated soils and sooner or later you end up badly in need of detoxification and feeling only half alive.

Life Mysteries

The secret to eating for rejuvenation is choosing wholesome foods – ones that are radiant with life energy – to increase mental and physical vitality, help restore hormonal order and re-establish biochemical balance. Raw fruits and vegetables have a remarkable ability to detoxify the body and enhance cell functions. So can naturally fermented foods such as miso. They help protect from free radical damage and improve the quality of micro-flora in the intestines. Green foods too have an important role to play. For life feeds upon life. And from a bio-chemical viewpoint when you think of life, think of enzymes.

Enter the Heroes

Enzymes are essential biochemical factors which govern our lives and our health. *Indogenous* enzymes – that is enzymes within our bodies – control virtually every biochemical process. *Exogenous* enzymes – also important – come to us from outside our bodies. They are found in fresh raw fruits and vegetables (more about these beasts in a moment). Many scientists refer to enzymes as 'the fountains of life' with good reason.

Within the human body it is enzymes which begin life, maintain life, and eventually bring life to an end. They are responsible for joining together chains of amino acids and enabling cell replication to take place. They support our immune system and protect us from harmful elements in our environment. They digest our foods and absorb our nutrients. They make it possible for us to breathe, move, and use our senses. Enzymes are necessary for such commonplace tasks as coagulating blood when we cut ourselves and for eliminating waste products from the body. Enzymes are even necessary for us to think or dream. Anti-oxidant enzymes, such as *glutathione-peroxidase* and *catalase*, play powerful roles in protecting us from ageing.

Very special and highly specific proteins, enzymes carry a kind of elemental energy – or basic life-force – which doctors working in natural medicine have long valued and worked with and which will never be measurable in chemical terms alone.

Let's Get Specific

When enzymes take action to modify, accelerate, or retard every metabolic function, they do this in a unique step-by-step manner which is highly economical and demands little energy. Each enzyme has evolved to help living organisms perform a specific task. Each enzyme also has its own life-span. When its mission is completed it ages and is then dismantled by other enzymes to be replaced afresh. Together they orchestrate a magnificent organic symphony whose purpose is to create perfect harmony in our bodies – preserving health and monitoring a remarkably complex system of checks and balances.

How well your body's enzymic systems work determines how close you come to living 'in the zone'. When a body is youthful and in good health a continuous supply of new enzymes are at hand to keep it working smoothly. Your biological age can be largely determined by your enzyme functions. The more vital they are the more vital you will be. A major factor in rejuvenating the body is rejuvenating the vitality of its enzymes. The body's indogenous enzymes can be easily destroyed, especially when we follow a lifestyle that is not really health-promoting: smoking, getting excessive ultra-violet light, using drugs, being exposed to radiation or to toxic substances.

Youth Factors

Enzyme quality is vastly improved by good diet and lifestyle. Enzymes need a good supply of specific minerals and vitamins for them to carry out their work. These essential nutrients such as vitamin B6, zinc, and magnesium are called *co-factors*. They come to us from our foods. Unless they are present in sufficient quantities, our enzymes cannot do their jobs and eventually the metabolic systems they govern break down so that degeneration takes place. The better the quality of the foods you eat, the better support you bring your body. But it is not only the co-factor nutrients found in the foods we eat that matter, but also the exogenous enzymes that foods contain.

Life Ingredients

Raw foods such as fresh vegetables, fruits, seeds and nuts are rich in exogenous enzymes. These food enzymes help us break down what we eat into nutrients for assimilation into the bloodstream. When they do not enter the body in sufficient quantities through what we eat, then the body's own enzymes have to work overtime to make up the difference. If this goes on day after day, year after year, the digestive system becomes less and less efficient. Then the body also has to call on more and more of its stored basic building blocks – amino acid chains, vitamins, minerals, and trace elements – to get the job done. It steals these nutrients from its own tissues and organs which need them for their other chores. All of this can result in a shortfall of the body's basic 'life ingredients' and a decrease in vitality.

Experts in enzyme biochemistry insist that a shortfall of enzymes is a major underlying cause in the development of degenerative diseases – from emphysema and osteoporosis, to gastro-intestinal disorders, Alzheimer's disease, osteoarthritis, and more serious illnesses including the auto-immune diseases like collagen diseases, rheumatoid arthritis, lupus (an ulcerous skin disease), scleroderma (a chronic hardened condition of the skin), and cancer. Rejuvenation demands that the body's enzymes be regenerated. Nothing will do this as efficiently as a high-raw diet.

Outside Help

Raw foods, rich in enzymes, not only help facilitate good digestion but aid the body's other metabolic activities as well. For a long time scientists assumed that enzymes in the foods we eat, being themselves proteins, would be completely broken down in the gut to become part of the amino acid pool from which we build new proteins. They insisted that the body was unable to absorb these exogenous enzymes directly. Now we know different. The latest enzyme research shows quite clearly that enzymes taken in from raw foods are absorbed to a significant degree as *macro-molecules* in biologically active form. Many are drawn through the wall of the gut directly into the bloodstream.

Enzymes such as *pancreatin*, *trypsin*, *chymotrypsin*, *amylase*, and *papain*, present in foods we eat, are absorbed into the bloodstream to varying degrees to aid digestion and support the body in many other ways – from counteracting viruses, inflammation and ageing, to enhancing immune function. Just how many enzymes you absorb depends on a number of different things and is constantly changing. Generally the more you need then the more of them you will absorb. Researchers find for instance that when an animal's immune system is suppressed it tends to absorb more enzymes than when it is functioning normally, presumably because its body so desperately needs help in order to carry out its functions.

Living Foods

Because enzymes help unlock the nutrients that we take in through our foods, making them available through the bloodstream to our cells, a high-raw, enzyme-rich diet becomes enormously important in helping to maintain the integrity and structure of collagen and elastin in the body. An abundance of enzymes and the nutrients that act as co-factors for them helps strengthen and improve the elasticity of arteries, veins, and capillaries. It also helps keep skin smooth as the years go by. Conversely enzyme deficiencies in the diet can result in the loss of skin tone, muscle tone and elasticity. Exogenous enzymes also help prevent *cross-linking* of collagen and enhance the blood supply to the dermis, the skin's deeper layers, keeping skin supple and radiant. And they improve the circulation of nutrients to the cells throughout the body, including the brain, as well as the elimination of wastes. Finally, enzymes are important in countering the build-up of toxic wastes in the intestines and elsewhere – what Dr Koda calls shukuben. As living things, food enzymes are easily destroyed by cooking and processing. This is one reason why raw foods become so important to rejuvenating the body.

Life In – Waste Out

Human evolution is a slow process. For hundreds of generations our ancestors lived on wild foods gathered and eaten raw. Our genes are specially adapted to dealing with raw foods. This is probably why raw foods have been so successfully used by experts in natural medicine to support healing, heighten vitality, and regenerate and rejuvenate.

More than sixty years ago Hans Eppinger, chief doctor at the First Medical Clinic of the University of Vienna, discovered that a high-raw way of eating leads to increased cellular respiration, eliminates accumulated wastes and toxins from cells and tissues, and supplies nutrients essential for optimal cell function. Perhaps most important of all, high-raw eating heightens the *micro-electrical tensions* – the life energies at a cellular level – associated with cell vitality, so that even cells in a particularly sluggish and neglected system are revitalized. They become better able to burn calories in the presence of oxygen, while at the same time protecting the body from free radical damage and producing energy for vitality and for carrying out the housekeeping on which continuing youthful functioning depends.

Micro-Magic

Capillaries are minute blood vessels which form the vast network of microcirculation throughout your body. It is their responsibility to deliver oxygen-rich blood for use in the cells. So important are these fine vessels that nature has supplied you with incredible lengths of them. If you were to attach all the capillaries in your body end to end they would measure some 60,000 miles in length – more than twice around the world. The state of your capillaries also determines to a great extent the functional age and condition of your body as a whole. For these transport systems are the arbitrators of cell nutrition, respiration and elimination. It is through these capillaries that nutrients and oxygen are carried to the cells all over the body – organs, skin, brain and glands – and wastes eliminated. Without good microcirculation, metabolism cannot take place efficiently.

Over the years the capillaries of people living on the average Western diet of highly processed foods (replete with junk fats, sugar and refined fare) become twisted, distended and highly porous. When this happens, proteins seep through and deposit themselves between the tissues and the capillary walls where they interfere with proper oxygen exchange and impede nutrient delivery and waste elimination. This can gradually starve cells, tissues and organs of all they need to function properly and can also lower cellular metabolic activity. The same degenerative process underlies the build-up of cellulite in women.) Such changes in microcirculation can not only lower overall vitality – since none of your body's parts are receiving oxygen and nutrients they need for healthy metabolic functions – but also predispose us to degenerative illness and to rapid ageing. A high-raw way of eating helps restore normal microcirculation.

Cell Tensions

The interchange of chemicals and energy between the microcirculation and the cells takes place through two thin membranes and a fine interstitial space. It happens only because the cells and capillaries have what is known as 'selective capacity'. This means they are able to absorb the substances they need and to reject what is harmful or unnecessary for metabolic processes. This selective capacity is the result of antagonistic chemical and micro-electrical tensions in the cells and tissues of all living systems. The stronger the tensions, the more intense these antagonisms, and the healthier and more vital your cells and your body as a whole will be and the more efficiently it will function.

Eppinger and another German scientist, Karl Eimer, discovered that a high-raw diet steadily *increases* the cells' selective capacity by heightening electrical potentials between tissue cells and capillary blood. This too improves the ability of your capillaries to regulate the transport of nutrients. It also helps detoxify the system, removing any 'sticky marsh' of waste products present – another factor encouraging the build-up of cellulite. A way of eating high in living foods – where, say, 50% of what you eat is taken raw – makes detox-ification, the improvement in the selective capacity of cells, the rebuilding of the body's enzymic systems, and metabolic rejuvenation as a whole, a straightforward occurrence.

De-Ageing Ferments

Fermented foods are also important for rejuvenation and age-protection. No people understand their value better than the Japanese. Unlike our high-tech food processing which fragments our foods and distorts their ability to support health, the Japanese traditions of slow, natural food processing and preservation used to create their staple foods like miso, kuzu, umeboshi, and brown rice vinegar actually improve a food's health-giving quality by enhancing its *chi* – its bio-energy (more about this in the next chapter). Traditional miso is made by combining *kogi* – cultured grain (or soybeans) which have been fermented – with plain soybeans, salt and water and then letting the whole ferment naturally for from three months to two years. Miso has potent anti-oxidant abilities. It has been shown to protect the body against radiation. And miso contains dipicolonic acid, an alkaloid which eliminates heavy metals from the body – including radioactive strontium. At Hiroshima University's Atomic Radioactivity Medical Laboratory, Professor Akihiro Ito tested miso's ability to protect against cancer in animals, and found it to be considerable.

Incorporating what may be initially unfamiliar ingredients such as miso, kuzu, brown rice vinegar, tofu, seaweeds and naturally fermented condiments such as umeboshi plums into your diet can not only enhance your health, help rebalance hormones, and aid rejuvenation, it can also bring wonderful variety to your meals.

'Good Guy' and 'Bad Guy' Bugs

Another major rejuvenating and health-enhancing aspect of naturally fermented foods is that, like a diet rich in fresh grains, fruits and vegetables but low in meat and free of dairy products, they help improve the quality and balance of our energy-supporting, anti-ageing intestinal flora. Researchers working on the China-Cornell-Oxford Diet and Health Project report that a diet of grains, vegetables and fruit improves the quality of bacteria that we have in the gut.

Each of us has between four and five hundred different kinds of bacteria in our intestines. Some, like the *bifido-bacteria*, are 'good guy' micro-organisms. They enhance immunity, control any overgrowth of negative organisms such as candida, and help protect against premature ageing and degenerative conditions like arthritis and cancer. The good guys feed heartily and develop in good number when fed certain natural sugars in plant foods and naturally fermented and soya-based products.

Other bacteria, such as the flora from the *Clostridium* family, are 'bad guys'. They proliferate when we eat a lot of meat and other animal foods including dairy products. Scientists working in the fascinating new field of *gastrointestinal ecology* are turning up more evidence every day that while bad-guy bacteria promote early ageing and degeneration, the good guys help reverse them. One way we can start to rejuvenate our bodies is by beginning to make shifts from a predominance of bad guy intestinal flora to a predominance of good guy ones. Naturally fermented foods and a high-raw diet rich in fresh vegetables, fruits and fibre from pulses and grains will do this automatically over time.

The Bones Have It

The latest research also shows that this way of eating reduces the likelihood of osteoporosis developing. Although Oriental people eat only half the calcium that Americans do, they have almost no osteoporosis. In part this is due to the fact that a diet high in meat and fish, eggs and dairy products such as Westerners are used to eating tends to be acid-forming. When these foods are eaten the body tends to counteract the build-up of acidity by leaching calcium from its bones and teeth in order to rebalance the *pH* of the blood. In China a mere 7% of protein ingested comes from animal sources, whereas between 60 and 70% of our proteins in the West are of animal origin. Vegetable-based proteins are alkaline-forming rather than acid-forming. They protect against calcium loss from the bones.

Superfoods Go Green

Like natural ferments, the green foods too have almost magical powers when it comes to de-ageing the body. The old adage 'eat your greens if you want to stay young and healthy' has become scientific fact. Recently an overwhelming abundance of medical and scientific evidence has come to the fore that dark green vegetables such as broccoli, Brussels sprouts, collards, kale, kohlrabi and mustard greens can help prevent cancer. The sulphur and histidine in brassicas detoxify the system of poisonous environmental chemicals and increase the body's own supply of natural cancer-fighting compounds. These foods also help lower LDL – *bad* cholesterol – and improve elimination. Clean Sweep, and the ongoing way of eating of which it is just the beginning, includes many green foods, since what protects against cancer protects also against degeneration and helps de-age the body.

What makes green plants green is *chlorophyll* – the substance in plants which converts the energy of the sun into chemical energy through the mysterious process of photosynthesis. This is no mean feat. All life on earth draws its power for life from the sun's energy thanks to photosynthesis in plants. Quite simply we would not be alive without it. The powers of chlorophyll for de-ageing the body are remarkable. In many experiments chlorophyll has been shown to protect animals from gene mutations associated with cancer that can arise through exposure to dangerous chemicals such as *benzopyrene* and *methylcholanthrene*. It is also known to inhibit the carcinogenic effects of exposure to simpler environmental poisons such as coal dust, tobacco, and to foods such as red wine and fried beef. In fact chlorophyll used on its own for these purposes has been proved to be more effective than the anti-oxidant vitamins A, C and E. Simple chlorophyll also inhibits the growth of bad-guy bacteria by creating an environment in which they simply do not reproduce. It also decreases swelling, reduces inflammation and speeds wound healing.

Take Grass

Cereal grasses are some of the least known but most potent rejuvenating green foods. Young grasses are very different from the mature grains they turn into. When rice, wheat, corn, oats, barley, rye or millet are grown in healthy soils and harvested at just the right time – 8–15 days after planting, just before *jointing* – they are unbelievably rich in vitamins and minerals, enzymes and growth hormones. The young germinated plant is a little miracle of nature. In the young leaves photosynthesis produces simple sugars which are transformed into proteins, fatty acids and nucleic acids such as DNA and RNA as well as complex carbohydrates. The young leaves are also abundant in chlorophyll which has an uncanny similarity in its chemical structure to *haemoglobin* – the oxygen carrier in the blood.

Japanese research scientist Yoshihide Hagiwara, exploring the nutritional powers of cereal grasses, concluded that 'the leaves of cereal grasses provide the nearest thing to the perfect food that this planet offers'. Other Japanese scientists working with barley grass have recently isolated an interesting protein – *P4–D1* – which has been found to protect cells from ultra-violet radiation and from specific cancer-causing substances. They believe this may be the result of the protein's ability to stimulate the repair of DNA, which helps at least in part to explain the remarkable rejuvenating properties of young cereal grasses.

Go Wild

You can find some of the very best of the green foods in your own back garden. These are weeds – dandelion, ragweed and lamb's quarters, for instance. They are intensely rich in minerals, trace elements, and rejuvenating green plant factors. Weeds are deep feeders and can absorb all sorts of goodness that shorter rooted crops have no access to. Seaweeds, too, are full of trace elements such as boron, chromium, cobalt, calcium, iodine, magnesium, manganese, molybdenum, phosphorus, potassium and silicon, all of which the body needs only in minute quantities but which are essential for efficient metabolism and youthful functioning.

Arguably the finest of all green foods are the algaes. Spirulina, a near-microscopic, blue-green freshwater algae, is one of the most important plant-based nutritional supplements you can use to support health and rejuvenation. Its protein is alkaline-forming – important for detoxification – and it is rich in vitamins E, B_{12}, C, B_1, B_5 and B_6 as well as beta carotene, zinc, copper, manganese, and selenium, important for rebuilding the system and for long-term anti-oxidant protection. Chlorella, a green algae which gets its name from its high chlorophyll content, is also good. It is rich in vitamins, minerals, fibre, nucleic acids, amino acids, and the all-important enzymes. Even better are the very best green superfood supplements which combine cereal grasses and algae with herbs, immune-enhancing mushrooms and other phyto-chemicals which have been formulated both for their biochemical properties and their energetics.

Take Life By Storm

Although explanations about how foods can be used for rejuvenation may seem complex, using them is pretty simple. The first step is forsaking convenience foods, with all their fragmentation and hidden fat and sugar, for a life-generating way of eating – one that is based on simple wholesome foods grown on healthy soils and eaten fresh and as close as possible to the state in which they come out of the ground. Incorporate a high degree of fresh vegetables and fruits, seeds and grains in your menus – as many of them eaten raw as possible. Finally, try to choose many of your foods from those rich in health-enhancing phyto-chemicals such as concentrated green foods, and naturally fermented foods from the Orient. The Clean Sweep diet will show you how to start exploring life at the peak of health and wellbeing while triggering an ongoing process of natural rejuvenation. Read on.

Step 5
Quantum Energy

NOW we come to the exciting stuff – energy. This is where life breaks all the rules. Biological science is just beginning to penetrate the mysteries of life energies. For thousands upon thousands of years, until now, they have remained the province of mystics and sages.

When it comes to rejuvenating the body, energy is where it's at. Put simply, successful rejuvenation depends on being able to activate energies which support the life force within. It is this life force that governs growth, nourishes us, sustains us, deep cleanses our bodies, regenerates our cells, heals us and makes us feel grateful just to be alive.

Buffalo and Daffodils

This ineffable life force is found in abundance in each of us as it is in all living things from buffalo to daffodils. Different cultures call it by different names. The Indians speak of it as *prana*. In Polynesia it is know as *mana*. The Chinese call it *chi*. All of these words describe various forms of subtle energy which until the advent of quantum physics remained largely unknown to Western science. Yet throughout history all forms of traditional medicine from Paracelsus to Chinese and Ayurvedic herbalism have worked with it.

Biophotons and Quantum Magic

Long ago quantum physicists established that wave particles such as electrons, atoms and molecules in living systems behave as *biophoton* energies. These biophoton or life energies appear to help regulate and control enzyme activities, cell reproduction and other activities in living systems. Experiments such as those reported in the March 1995 issue of *Scientific American* by Brumer and Shapiro have established the existence of these particle/wave reactions in organisms. Like light bulbs, atoms give out radiant bio-energies which can either act constructively or destructively on the body's own molecules. Scientists are beginning to define how the interference wave forms generated both by internally manufactured toxins and by environmental pollutants act. Their effect on the body can be destructive, interfering with the harmonious biophoton energies on which health and protection from premature ageing depend, or constructive, supporting health and vitality. Within the next decade we are going to hear a lot more about these biophoton energies and their effects on our health. Right now we can still make practical use of existing knowledge about how to influence them for healing and regeneration.

Energy Consciousness

From the point of view of quantum physics, as human beings we are not only immersed in an energy field, our bodies, our minds and our selves *are* energy fields. These fields are constantly expanding, contracting and changing as our thoughts, diet and lifestyle change. The aim of any form of natural treatment, from dietary change and detoxification to hydrotherapy, exercise and meditation is firstly to enhance *positive bio-energies* in an organism and secondly to help to balance them and create order.

Many researchers now work with bio-energies and the kind of transformations they can bring about. Medical intuitives such as Caroline Myss – international lecturer on human consciousness – are capable of clairvoyantly examining subtle energy states in a person and of pinpointing where his or her bio-energies are being dissipated. In doing this Myss helps people learn to work with their own bio-energies to bring about self-healing.

Etheric Forces

Chromatography is a useful tool for studying energy. It is widely used in chemistry, biology, medicine and industry as a way of analysing complex substances such as the amino acids in a protein or for detecting impurities in a compound. The use of chromatography to measure energy differences between living things and between natural and synthetically made substances was originally developed by European chemist Ehrenfreid Pfeiffer.

Early on in his career Pfeiffer was asked by the German mystic Rudolph Steiner to find a chemical reagent that could be useful in charting the quality of life energy – what Steiner called the *formative etheric forces* – in living matter. After experimenting with many different substances Pfeiffer discovered that when he added extracts of living plants to a solution of copper chloride and then let it evaporate slowly it would produce a beautiful pattern of crystallization typical of the species of plant used. Radiant form and shape consistently indicated the life strength of the plant. Pfeiffer established that strong crystallization patterns indicated health, while weak ones indicated ill-health.

Sheer Radiance

More recently, in university parapsychology research laboratories such as the one at UCLA in California, scientists like Dr Thelma Moss have experimented with techniques such as Kirlian photography to examine, record and analyze the unique energetic patterns living things emanate. Kirlian photography is one of the methods whereby ordinarily non-visible force-fields around and through living and non-living things can be recorded visually and studied. Kirlian photographs are extraordinarily beautiful. Researchers find they get consistent results when working with the Kirlian method to photograph plants and foods, for instance when comparing cooked foods with their raw counterparts, or the leaf of a healthy plant with the leaf of a damaged one. Kirlian photography enables the luminescent energy corona from a living thing to be recorded on film. Healthy plants or super-foods such as organically grown herbs, wild 'crafted' algae, organic green juices, and plant enzymes have significantly stronger, more radiant and wider coronas than do processed foods. The corona produced by properly harvested spirulina or an organic raw carrot or cauliflower is dramatically reduced when these foods are cooked or processed. Uncooked vegetables and fruits radiate brilliant spikes of light, harmoniously surrounded by geometric shapes. Cooked and processed foods show only the dimmest evidence of corona discharge. Foods, plants and herbs with a wide corona carry a lot of the life energy useful for rejuvenation.

Nowadays scientists working with techniques like

chromatography, Kirlian photography, photomicrography and polarized light field photography – as well as clairvoyant healers who can actually 'see' changes in energy patterns around plants, people and animals – confirm that certain foods, herbs and plant products carry high levels of harmonious bio-energy. They can be used to enhance the beauty of a living organism's energy patterns. So can techniques of breathing, meditation and deep relaxation, as well as the laying on of hands or spiritual healing, hydrotherapy, bodywork and autogenics. That is why all of these things can be so helpful in the rejuvenation process.

Healing the Impossible

One of the most interesting researchers to look into the area of life force treatments for healing and regeneration is the American healer Mitchell May. At the age of 22 May was in a car accident that profoundly damaged him. He lost several inches of bone from his legs, and the tissue and nerve damage was extensive. He lay in insufferable pain. His physicians told him he would never walk again and that it was necessary to have his right leg amputated. They also informed him that his immune system would be permanently compromised and that his health would be severely restricted for the rest of his life.

May was lucky enough to have been hospitalized at one of the most important medical research centres in the world, the University of California Medical Centre at Los Angeles. There he became part of a special study involving ongoing experiments into life force healing and extra-sensory perceptions using skilled spiritual healers working under strict scientific controls. He met and worked with a very gifted healer named Jack Gray. Gray's great gift was his ability to activate powerful and natural healing life force energies within a person. Within a week of Gray having begun simple laying-on-of-hands treatment, May discovered he was able to turn off and on his experience of excruciating pain using the techniques taught him by Gray.

Energy Healing

May became fascinated with the whole area of life force healing and became an apprentice to Gray. He developed an interest in states of consciousness, in subtle energy and in discovering ways to enhance life force through the use of spiritual healing, plant foods and biological compounds that have a particularly high quality of energetic radiation. May's own story is one of the most well documented tales of 'impossible' recovery in medical annals. Not only did his body heal, he was able to learn to walk again and now, almost 25 years later, he has full use of his body. In the process he has also become one of the most respected and acclaimed healers in the world.

During the period of his recovery May worked intimately with Gray and with Thelma Moss in her parapsychology research laboratory at UCLA, photographing energy patterns around foods and other nutritional substances. He also carried out wide searches of scientific literature and conferred with physicists, health professionals, doctors and practitioners of natural medicine, both those trained in Western science and those whose skills had developed within Oriental health traditions. He set out to discover, test and record information about specific foods and plant compounds which can enhance human health – not only chemically by supplying an abundance of vitamins, minerals, phyto-anti-oxidants and immune-enhancers, but also by providing an abundance of life force. May wanted to find ways of making it possible to help people live at their fullest energy, vitality and wholeness, in maximum health and wellbeing.

Entranced by Beauty

Before long May became totally fascinated by the beauty of energy patterns certain foods and plants emitted. He also became convinced – as have many researchers both before and since – that the fundamental processes of healing and rejuvenation depend on intensifying the life force within an individual and then helping to bring about a harmonization and balance of its movements within the living system. He saw that there was so much potential to help people by working in an energetic way. He also discovered (as have practitioners of natural medicine) that it is not just food and plants that are able to enhance the life force. He experimented with many forms of meditation and breathing, shifts in attitudes of mind, and various healing modalities and energy-shifting exercise, such as Tai-Chi, yoga and the martial arts, which enable us to awaken the life force within.

Most of all, he loved working with plants. Through his work he identified plants, algae, mushrooms, sprouted seeds and grains, all of which carry an abundance of this life energy. He also found they could be used to intensify a person's own life energy and help create coherent and harmonious patterns of energy within. As early researchers into the healing effects of living foods such as Dr Max Bircher-Benner and Dr Max Gerson had insisted, plants are holders and emitters of *quantum sunlight* – life force which we can use to our advantage, either taken fresh and live or when harvested and dried properly. These plants are able to transfer their life force to us.

Perfect Balance

May's highly practical experiments were carried out over twenty years, during which he conferred with the finest practitioners in Western medicine as well as experts in Chinese and Ayurvedic medicine, and also with spiritual healers. Slowly, painstakingly, he was able to identify organically grown foods and plants with a particular abundance of life force and to develop ways of further heightening their powers for healing by combining them in a carefully formulated synergetic way, so that the energies of each balanced and enhanced the energies of the others. Out of this he developed what I believe to be the most remarkable and potent nutritional supplement that I have ever come across. It is called Pure Synergy. Its combination of sixty-two of nature's most potent and nourishing ingredients include organically grown freeze-dried herbs, organically grown immune-supporting mushrooms, plant enzymes, freeze-dried royal jelly, wild crafted algae, organic green juices and many other natural elements, and is the finest superfood you can get (see Resources).

Energetic Rejuvenation

May, and others like him such as Dr David Peat and (twice) Nobel nominee Robert O Becker have delved deeply into the field of subtle energy. They are helping to build bridges between orthodox, chemically-based, *allopathic* medicine (which until recently paid little attention to the energetic aspects of healing) and the ancient traditions of medicine which have always viewed healing as primarily an energy art. Breathing, movement, thoughts and dreams as well as the metabolism of the foods that we eat all contribute to active energy 'information' or life 'intelligence' capable of bringing about a continuous circulation of harmonious energy to transform and heal the body. Energetically speaking, illness and degeneration are viewed as some sort of misalignment or blockage which interferes with the natural flow of energy, perverting its natural balance or siphoning energy off from its natural vital function of supporting the body. Rejuvenation takes place by using everything at one's disposal to enhance this harmonious and orderly circulation of life energy. The dynamic harmony within body/mind, and the restoration of energetic balance which energy-based rejuvenation aims to bring about, is not a static state but a *dynamic* process, whereby energy continually circulates and health continually unfolds. This is living 'in the zone' at its very best. This in turn helps bring about a process of renewal, regeneration and expansion of the individual spirit and its life purpose. After all, everything each of us needs to regenerate and rejuvenate ourselves lies *within*.

Pure Alchemy

There are no magic bullets for rejuvenation. What works is creating a lifestyle for yourself that continues to support your energetic flow at a very high level. Based on long-standing principles of natural healing, *The 10-Day Plan* offers a combination of synergistic practices to help you do just that. It too creates a synergy, the whole becoming far greater than the sum of its parts. The aim is to create mental, physical and spiritual harmony, to help you gather and set free the life force that dwells within you and to awaken your latent potential for vitality, creativity and joy.

The Chinese, who have probably delved into the whole process of rejuvenation more than any other culture, consider the whole process an alchemical one. They see it as a great art *and* science in which ultimately a person becomes more fully who he or she truly is, living out his or her physical, emotional, mental and spiritual potential to the full. To put it another way, rejuvenation is a process in which 'base metal' undergoes a remarkable series of transformations first by being broken down into its *materia prima* (here's where detoxification comes in) and then transformed into 'gold'. This alchemical process, which is also recognized by the Sufi and Ayurvedic traditions, not only occurs on a level of external and material change, promoting the development of a younger, stronger, healthier body, but also on a spiritual, psychological level whereby the soul, the heart and the head are united together with the material body in what is traditionally referred to as a 'mystical marriage'.

Urgent Needs

At this point in history we have a greater need than ever to learn to practise such alchemy within ourselves. Our air and water have become polluted. There is less and less quality fresh food readily available. Much of the food that is used is poisoned by herbicides and pesticides which distort bodily processes, polluting our bodies and undermining our clarity of thought and visions in ways that can seriously interfere with our ability to maintain health on a physical and spiritual level. Only we can change that for ourselves. I believe it is time we began to turn away from the whole idea of magic bullets, symptomatic treatments and quick-fix ideas, replacing them with foods and natural techniques that enhance our energies and support our lives in the best possible ways. Once the life force energy is built the body heals itself. *The 10-Day Plan* begins the process.

THE
PLAN

Step 6
Clean Sweep

Rejuvenation begins with a 10-day *total being* mind-body-spirit detox programme designed to eliminate stored wastes and revitalize cells and systems. Thanks to the way it is designed, during this period you will also begin the process of regenerating tissues and rebuilding your metabolic system – restoring more youthful functions all round.

Organic Miracles

All rejuvenation comes from within. The capacity of the body to regenerate itself is one of the miracles inherent in every organic system. Yet it never ceases to amaze me each time I see it happen. Within this first 10 days you will already reap enormous benefits. The programme can firm your flesh, smooth your skin, make your eyes brighter, and help clear stress, both physical and emotional. It can also teach you some powerful and positive habits that will continue the process of de-ageing long afterwards. If you continue to choose to follow a de-ageing lifestyle you could well reach a level of wellbeing and energy you have not experienced before.

The 10-Day Plan has four cornerstones.

- Clean Sweep Diet (just what it says)
- Psychic Scrub: (detoxification for the inner being)

- Hydro Electrics: (water power at its best)
- Reinventing The Body: (total rejuvenation through movement)

Together they form the foundations of an ongoing lifestyle for continual de-ageing.

The New Detox

Let's look at Clean Sweep Diet. Detox has become the buzzword of the Nineties. Yet inner cleansing is hardly something new. Detoxification has been used for millennia as a way of healing and rejuvenation. From the sweat lodges of Native Americans and the herbal treatments of the Amazon Indians to the juice fasts of the Europeans, detoxifying the body forms the basis of all forms of natural healing.

Some detox programmes involve fasting on water or juice. Others use high-raw or all-raw diets or mono diets where you eat nothing for a specific period except, say, brown rice. Fasting is the most powerful way to detox. By now scores of animal studies have shown that periodic fasting extends life. Fasting has been shown to decrease the rate of free radical generation and to inhibit the production of damaging crosslinking compounds in the body. In highly complex ways fasting can both slow down and help reverse ageing. As fasting expert Joel Fuhrman, author of *Fasting For Health*, says, 'Fasting, by blunting most physiological mechanisms of ageing, dismantles immune system imbalances that contribute to disease.'

The trouble with fasting is that it is an extreme method of detox. To carry it out you need to work with a doctor or a highly trained health practitioner. It is also most certainly something that no-one should attempt on their own. On a fast where you are drinking nothing but water it is virtually impossible to continue to work and live your ordinary life. Far too much of the body's energies are taken up in profound physiological cleansing to allow daily activities.

Help When You Need It

Clean Sweep Diet comes to the rescue of ordinary people who want the benefits of detoxification but have neither the time nor the desire to set their life aside for it to happen. Clean Sweep brings the same deep inner cleansing of a fast, but it works more slowly, more gently and without risk. Like fasting too, it calls on time-tested principles of inner-cleansing, yet it marries them with cutting-edge scientific discoveries which enable us to deep cleanse the system with a maximum of efficiency and a minimum of discomfort.

Recently orthodox scientists have been examining the process of detoxification in an attempt to understand just how it performs its many 'miracles': healing, heightening mental clarity, re-establishing emotional balance and raising vitality. Working together with clinical physicians and researchers around the world, experts like Jeffrey Bland and his colleagues at the HealthComm International Research Centre in the United States have carried out collaborative studies into the effects that diet and lifestyle exert on the body's age-protective systems – its anti-oxidant capacities and immune regulation. Their work confirms what experts in natural healing have claimed for two millennia: that following a detox programme impacts positively on the body, spurring on the healing of patients with long-term ailments including chronic fatigue syndrome, heart disease, arthritis, irritable bowel disorder, and many other acute and chronic illnesses, as well as helping to clear mental and emotional disturbances. They also discovered that the detoxification of steroid wastes including the *xenobiotics* – the toxic substances such as petroleum-based herbicides, pesticides, and plastics which are disturbing male and female reproductive systems and which we take in through food, air and water (see Chapter Ten) – takes place in *two* distinct stages.

Nature Knows

During Stage I a group of super-enzymes known as *cytochrome P450*s activate fat-soluble poisons in the body – like pesticides and herbicides that have destructive oestrogenic effects – and emulsify them in the body's fluids. During Stage II another series of enzymes attach to these dissolved toxins and remove them from the system.

For a detox diet to be both effective and easy your body needs to be well supplied with compounds that support both Stage I and Stage II enzymes. You will need *inulin*, for instance, which enhances the production of certain fatty acids that regenerate the mucosa in the gut and support cellular energy production; also vitamins, minerals, and trace elements such as molybdenum and potent plant factors to activate anti-oxidant activity. Where do you find such elements?

There are two ways to go. You can take a complex nutritional supplement such as the one Jeff Bland formulated called Ultra Clear. It is a product which boasts high levels of anti-oxidant nutrients like *n-acetylcysteine* that act against free radicals generated during the detoxification process as well as others that support cytochrome P450 and other enzymic actions. Such a formula will do the job but it too requires the participation of a health professional to use it. The other way to go is to get all the support you need for both Stage I and Stage II detox from natural foods while leaning heavily on green plant factors. This is the way Dr

Mitsuo Koda at the famous Koda Clinic in Osaka chooses to detox. And this is the way Clean Sweep Diet works. It is a natural food method you can do yourself.

Detox To Go

Clean Sweep is based on a high level of vegetables – especially green leaves – fruits, pulses and some grains, together with the addition of certain superfoods such as freeze-dried cereal grasses, seaweeds, blue-green algae, and natural ferments like miso. It uses no vitamin or mineral pills. The diet, in fact the whole 10-day programme, is designed to travel. You can go out to work, play tennis, go shopping or do pretty much anything else you usually do while your body carries out its work of inner-clearing. Here are a few of the things it can do for you:

Clean Sweep Benefits

Detoxification and Rebuilding

Clean Sweep doesn't just clear out the old, it helps to rebuild the body's metabolic systems – something most detox programmes do not even dream of doing. Where unbalanced detox programmes can deplete the body of critical nutrients, Clean Sweep brings you optimal supplies of both macro- and micro-nutrients to make the whole job easier and minimize cleansing reactions.

Anti-Ox Support

Clean Sweep supplies a superb balance of anti-oxidants, anti-cancer, anti-ageing and immune-supporting factors of the highest order – potent plant-based substances and compounds including *polyphenols*, *bioflavonoids* and *glucosinolates* found in cruciferous vegetables, ferrulic acid in rice, the alliums, all woven together by Nature in perfect synergy with proteins, vitamins, minerals and fatty acids in natural foods.

Energy Raising

The living foods which form the core of Clean Sweep vibrate with a special energy which even the most sophisticated manufactured nutritional supplements will never match. They will benefit you physically and mentally, helping to raise your energetic experience of aliveness and radiance to new levels of excellence.

Enzyme Boosting

The foods Clean Sweep uses and the nutrients they contain enhance digestive processes. This improves assimilation of important nutrients and other protective elements.

Sensitivity Banishing

Clean Sweep cuts out most common food allergens such as wheat, sugar and dairy products that cause sensitivity reactions in many people to pollute their system and lower vitality. This helps you to feel the surges of clarity and energy that come with detoxification much sooner.

10 Days to a New You

Like spring cleaning a house the beginning of any detoxification programme can be hard work for your body. It diverts life energies away from outer activities, turning them deep within where the important tissue cleansing and regenerative processes are gearing up. This is why it is best to begin Clean Sweep on a Friday. Then you have a weekend at the beginning during which you can get some extra rest the first two or three days as your system begins the work of cleansing itself. During the first few days, you may also need to give yourself a little more tender loving care than usual.

The 10-Day Plan is not some quick-fix pill one can pop. It requires a certain amount of dedication and discipline to carry out. You will have a lot of things to learn and practise in the next 10 days. Give yourself time to learn. Clear the decks in your life to make way for an experience that is potentially life-changing. *The Plan* can be a lot of fun but it is also serious business. If you intend to carry out the programme while you work then avoid making dates in the evening so you have plenty of time to practise the natural rejuvenation technologies. *The Plan* can be great if you have a partner to go through it with. You might even like to keep a journal day by day of your thoughts, experiences and changing perceptions. You may be surprised by the depth of the transformations it can bring about.

CLEAN SWEEP DIET

Breakfast Goes Green:

Breakfast each day is simple. You drink it. Everything you take in at breakfast time is raw and green.

The liver – the body's organ of inner cleansing – is most active between midnight and mid day. Raw fruits and vegetables, green foods such as spirulina and green formulas such as Pure Synergy support the liver's morning clear-out better than anything. Their digestion doesn't make demands on the liver so it can get on with the business at hand. It is also so easy that it demands only a tiny fraction of the energy you would need for cereals or scrambled eggs. Drink a big glass of whichever recipe you prefer (see Recipes,

p. 171) you prefer and add to it your rejuvenating greens. Choose from one of these:

- Energy Shake
- Fresh Fruit Juice
- Fresh Vegetable Juice

Gentle Into Green

If you have been used to a diet of convenience foods, you will probably want to begin slowly to introduce yourself to the green foods – whether this be by adding a handful of dandelion leaves, lettuce or spinach to your energy shake or spooning in some powdered spirulina, green barley or Pure Synergy. Green foods are about as far away from convenience foods as you can get. For some they take a little getting used to. The first energy shake you make you might want to add only a leaf or two of a green vegetable or as little as half a teaspoon of powdered green superfood.

Go easy when you go green. Don't even use greens for the first couple of days of the diet if you don't want to. As your body detoxifies you will not only find the greens easier to take, you are likely to end up loving them. Once this happens you can use as much as 250g (9 oz) of green leaf herbs and vegetables in an energy shake (or a big glass of fresh fruit or vegetable juice) or a heaped tablespoon of powdered green superfood. You may even come to love green so much that you will not even bother with fruit and vegetable juices to mix it with. You may prefer to do as I often do: stir a heaped tablespoon of Pure Synergy into a glass of spring water and drink it neat. This is particularly useful for travel.

During the ten days on Clean Sweep, lunch and dinner are interchangeable. The one will be a delicious whole-meal salad. The other is based on low-fat, high fibre dishes made from grains, pulses and vegetables. It doesn't matter which you choose to have when.

Super Salad Meal

This meal consists of a total-meal salad chock full of crunchy vegetables rich in rejuvenating plant factors. Choose five or more vegetables from the super salad list below, chop or shred them and put them into a bowl: cabbage, kale, fennel, chard, collards, lettuce, spinach, watercress, lamb's lettuce, rocket, radicchio, carrots, turnips, parsnips, radishes, beet-root, celery, yams, sweet potatoes, broccoli, cauliflower, peppers, tomatoes, swedes. Dress the salad with olive oil and lemon, season with fresh or dried herbs, tamari, and top with slices of tofu, flakes of nori seaweed, or seeds such as sunflower, pumpkin and sesame, or fresh raw chopped nuts such as hazels, pecans, almonds, walnuts or pines.

Grain and Veg Meal

This meal can be part cooked and part raw or all cooked. It can be a simple meal made up of a grain dish such as a bowl of brown rice or *kasha* together with steamed or stir-fried vegetables or pulse-based dishes such as lentil or split-pea soups with a slice or two of 100% rye bread or crispbread.

Water Magic

During the 10-Day Clean Sweep Diet it is important to drink plenty of clean water. A couple of glasses first thing in the morning and then more between meals throughout the day. Never drink at meal times nor less than 30 minutes before a meal or 2 hours afterwards. $1^1/_2$ to 2 litres (3 to 4 pints) a day is a good general guideline. The easiest way to do this is either to buy a 1¹/₂ litre (3 pints) bottle of mineral water or fill a 1¹/₂ to 2 litre (3 to 4 pints) container with clean water and make sure you empty it by the end of the day. You can use up some of your water quota by making herb tea if you prefer and miso broth which is an excellent way of calling the power of natural ferments into your rejuvenation programme.

Drink nothing else. No coffee, tea or alcohol during The 10-Day Plan. Clean Sweep is hypo-allergenic, that is, it eliminates the two most common foods that trigger sensitivities in most people: wheat and dairy products. And it is vegan. It uses no meat, fish or poultry. In can be fun to create your own meals following the Clean Sweep guidelines. Take a look at the menu plan below for inspiration and check out a few of the simple recipes it uses at the back of the book to get you started. Here are ten days of my own menus:

Leslie's Menu Plan

Day One: Friday

BREAKFAST (see Recipes, p. 171)
Pineapple and Blueberry Energy Shake with 100g (4 oz) dandelion and lamb's lettuce leaves

LUNCH
Brown Rice and Vegetable Risotto seasoned with tamari and spiked with wakami seaweed

DINNER
Winter Chunk Salad (see Recipes, p. 176)
with tofu mayonnaise (see Recipes, p. 175)

Day Two: Saturday

BREAKFAST
Fresh pressed carrot and apple juice with a heaped tablespoon of Pure Synergy

LUNCH
Grated carrot, red and white cabbage, fennel, and chopped celery salad topped with minced hazlenuts, parsley and mint, sprinkled with flakes of nori seaweed and dressed with lemon oil

DINNER
Wok fried vegetables and mixed sea plants, with tofu, served on soba (100% buckwheat noodles)

Day Three: Sunday

BREAKFAST
A heaped tablespoon of Pure Synergy in a glass of spring water

LUNCH
A bowl of kasha (see Recipes p.173) topped with steamed peas, carrots, courgettes, and seasoned with garlic and ginger

DINNER
Garden cruch salad (see Recipes p.173)

Day Four: Monday

BREAKFAST
Banana and Orange Energy Shake with 1 heaped tablespoon of spirulina

LUNCH
Lentil and vegetable soup with a slice of 100% rye bread

DINNER
Sprout Salad (see Recipes p.175) topped with diced tofu and dressed with olive oil and lemon, garlic and basil

Day Five: Tuesday

BREAKFAST
Fresh pressed apple juice spiked with ginger with 1 heaped tablespoon of powdered green barley

LUNCH
A bowl of Leek and Barley Soup made with wakami seaweed, carrots, celery, sweet potatoes, and arame seaweed

DINNER
Spinach salad with onions topped with carrots, celeriac, and red and yellow peppers sliced into matchsticks, sprinkled with chopped almonds and seasoned with garlic. Tofu vinaigrette dressing (see Recipes p.176)

Day Six: Wednesday

BREAKFAST
Watermelon juice with a heaped tablespoon of Pure Synergy

LUNCH
A bowl of polenta (see Recipes p.174) topped with wok fried onions, aubergine, courgettes and tomatoes, seasoned with oregano, cayenne pepper, spring onions, and garlic

DINNER
Watercress salad with cos lettuce, spring onions, courgettes, carrots and tomatoes, topped with sesame and pumpkin seeds and dressed with Wild Carrot Dressing (see Recipes p.176)

Day Seven: Thursday

BREAKFAST
Banana and apple Energy Shake plus a handful of lamb's lettuce and rocket

LUNCH
Barley Pilaff (see Recipes p.172) with baked parsnips, sweet potatoes and carrots

DINNER
Radicchio salad with celery, kombu seaweed that has been soaked in water for 15 minutes, mung-beans, chicory, cucumber, carrots and onions, dressed with olive oil and lemon and topped with chopped walnuts

Day Eight: Friday

BREAKFAST
Beetroot and apple juice with 1 heaped tablespoon of Pure Synergy

LUNCH
A bowl of brown rice topped with Russian Red Stir-Fry (see Recipes p.174)

DINNER
Summer salad of mixed vegetables dressed with tofu vinaigrette (see Recipes p.176)

Day Nine: Saturday

BREAKFAST
Grape and banana Energy Shake with a handful of mixed lettuce

LUNCH
All green salad made from broccoli, watercress, lamb's lettuce, rocket and soaked hiziki seaweed, topped with sunflower seeds and dressed with olive oil and lemon, garlic and ginger

DINNER
Vegetable soup with celery, parsnips, garden peas, runner beans, bay leaves, millet, garlic and miso topped with chopped parsley

Day Ten: Sunday

BREAKFAST
Papaya and Pineapple Energy Shake with a heaped table-spoon of Pure Synergy added

LUNCH
Red lentil and vegetable stew with onions, cauliflower, carrots, red pepper, broccoli and tomatoes, seasoned with turmeric, cumin, coriander and fresh ginger.

DINNER
A dish of crudités and a bowl of tofu dip (see Recipes p.175)

It's important to be prepared for the dynamic changes that can take place on Clean Sweep. When we begin to practise the techniques outlined later on in this book and to eat foods of a very high quality some pretty amazing changes start to happen, for all of these things activate life energies. The closer that food comes to its natural state, the more of the ineffable life force it carries, and the more capable it is of inducing profound alterations in the body. At the top of the list of life-enhancing foods are raw fruits, vegetables, sprouted seeds and grains, and the superfoods which include blue-green algae, chlorella and immune-stimulating mushrooms. What all of these foods have in common is that they have the ability to transport an abundance of life energy. When at the same time you increase your intake of them you also eliminate artificially stimulating substances such as coffee, tea, chocolate and tobacco, the amazing cellular intelligence of the body takes over and immediately becomes manifest. Because the quality of life energy coming into the body is higher than the quality of the tissues within the body itself, the system quickly begins to throw off lower-grade materials and tissue in order to create space for the superior life energies it uses to rejuvenate itself and to create healthier tissue.

Life Force In – Life Force Out

The more you fill the body with life energies, the more rapidly the process of throwing off waste matter and the elimination of less-than-healthy tissue takes place. As this happens you may experience what in natural medicine is know as a 'healing crisis'. Symptoms such as swelling, the odd cold, headache, or even temporary fatigue may appear as the body is readjusting itself away from artificial stimulants and eliminating toxins. During the elimination process this can be registered as discomfort.

You may even get a temporary feeling of let-down which can last for a day or two, especially at the beginning of the programme, where the heart, having been stimulated by caffeine and other irritants, begins to beat more slowly and the false exhilaration you used to experience from stimulants temporarily turns into a feeling of being down. Any initial let-down won't last long. In most people it never occurs at all. Yet it is important to be aware of the possibility should it happen to you and take extra care of yourself until it clears. Autogenic training (see Chapter seven), sleep, and simple rest will help you re-learn the art of self-care.

At the beginning of detoxification you may find too that the skin breaks out a bit, that your bowels become temporarily sluggish, or you have loose bowels. You may feel tired too, not much inclined to exercise. You can also find yourself urinating a lot more than usual. For most people any reactions to detoxification are minor. Each day they become more and more calm yet filled with energy. Gradually – bit by bit – you may discover that you look better and feel better than you have in years.

New Horizons

What I find exciting is not just the physical experiences that happen as the body de-ages – detoxification, stabilization and rebuilding – but their mental or spiritual counterparts. It is as though your mind opens up. You begin to see life with a much broader view. You can feel a sense of excitement each day with whatever you are doing, so that feelings of depression and impossibilities gradually melt away like snowdrifts in the warmth of spring sunshine. What you are experiencing are only your own life energies and your natural balanced state of mind emerging. At peace and centred, you are more and more able to do whatever it is you choose to do, no matter what your age or condition at the start.

The body is a magnificent system that is capable of the most incredible regeneration and renewal. Living on simple, pure, natural foods after you have finished Clean Sweep will offer your system the opportunity to transform itself and in the process to transform the whole person physically, emotionally and spiritually. A human being is truly 'fearfully and wonderfully made'.

Step 7
Psychic Scrub

When it comes to rejuvenation on an emotional and spiritual level the most powerful way there is to liberate life energy is simply to *tell the truth*. This means nothing more than allowing yourself to be what you are, without the pretensions or self-limiting assumptions that can unconsciously block the experience of being fully alive and able to make full use of your potentials. Far too much vitality lies still-born beneath patterns of addictive behaviour, fear, and heavy psychological baggage – the kind of stuff we all carry around with us to thwart our energy and make simply being who we are hard work.

Life Energy Thwarted

The physical, emotional, spiritual and social environment in which most of us grow up rarely supports the full unfolding of our individual nature. As a result, like a plant trying to develop in depleted soil with too little rain and not enough sun, each of us develops our own brand of disharmony and distortion. We may try to change ourselves to be what we think others want us to be, or to bury deep inside us all our fears, disappointments and frustrations lest they rock the boat of our day-to-day lives.

Every past experience, all our thoughts, perceptions and fears can become encoded within the molecular structures of the body in the form of layer after layer of old 'stress'. Later on in life such 'encoding' can manifest as muscle tension, metabolic processes that don't function as well as they should, negative thought patterns and recurring emotions such as fear, anxiety or depression.

This happens to all of us to some degree. When we carry around a lot of old stress we can also gradually develop a lack of trust in ourselves, a lack of confidence, or a feeling of being unworthy or guilty. We can even end up burdened by a sense of meaninglessness which leads to addiction, or greed for material things so that no matter how much we acquire we never fill up our emptiness.

Polishing the Lens of Perception

At the core, at the very centre of our being, beneath whatever physical, emotional or mental rubbish we have accumulated, is where true freedom is to be found. Rediscovering this freedom is essential for rejuvenation. It asks that we let go of distorted habit patterns, fears and frustrations which have developed over the years and gradually reassert our trust in our essential self. The false ideas, notions and habit patterns that suppress and squander our life energy make us highly susceptible to early ageing. They represent psychic and spiritual rubbish which is not only a big energy drainer but can cause as much free radical damage as living on junk food or taking drugs.

The wonderful thing about the psyche is that, like the body, given half the chance it will detoxify itself so that life-changing psychic and spiritual energy is released. Psychic detoxification brings a spiritual rejuvenation in its wake that can echo throughout your whole life adding the freshness of a child's vision to the wisdom you have developed over the years.

There are many ways to go about it. Good psychotherapy can help. So can meditation, certain energy approaches to exercise such as *Chi Chung*, Tai Chi, Yoga and martial arts practices – provided always that they are taught with a real understanding of the spiritual power that underlies them. But one of the simplest to learn yet most effective ways of cleaning the psyche is *autogenic training*. It costs nothing but a little time to learn the technique. Once learned, you can do it for five or ten minutes a day over time, and it will be of immense help in clearing away psychological blocks and lifting off stresses that have been locked deep within, often virtually for a lifetime.

Detox the Psyche

A thorough, comprehensive technique for relaxation and personal transformation, autogenic training was developed in the early 1930s by the German psychiatrist Johannes H Schultz. It consists of a series of simple mental exercises designed to turn *off* the body's 'fight or flight' mechanism and turn *on* the restorative rhythms and harmonizing associated with profound psychophysical relaxation. Practised daily, it can bring results comparable to those achieved by serious Eastern meditators. Yet unlike meditation, autogenics has no cultural, religious or cosmological overtones. It demands no special clothing, unusual postures or practices. When you practise autogenics emotional and spiritual detoxification happens in just the way physical detoxification occurs on Clean Sweep Diet, and once again the whole process is generated from *within*.

Freedom From Within

Johannes Schultz was a student of the clinically orientated neuro-pathologist Oskar Vogt, who at the turn of the century at the Berlin Neurological Institute was deeply involved in research on sleep and hypnosis. Vogt remarked that some of his patients who had been subjected to hypnosis developed the ability to put themselves in and out of a hypnotic state – or rather autohypnotic, since it was self-induced. These people experienced remarkable relief from tension and fatigue and also tended to recover from whatever psychosomatic disorders they had been suffering from. Drawing on Vogt's observations, Schultz went on to design techniques that would enable people to induce this deep mental and psychological relaxation at will.

Schultz found that when men and women enter the autohypnotic state they experience two specific physical phenomena: the first is a sensation of heaviness in the limbs and torso, and the second a feeling of diffuse warmth throughout the body. The sensation of heaviness is caused by deep relaxation in the body's muscles and the warmth is the result of vasodilation in the peripheral arteries. Schultz reasoned that if he taught people to suggest to themselves that these things were happening to their bodies they might rapidly and simply be able to experience a state of passive concentration which in turn would exert a positive influence over the *autonomic nervous system*, balancing energies of mind and body, helping the person experience a high level of relaxed vitality and freedom from premature degeneration, and gradually clearing away negative thought and behaviour patterns that have been interfering with the person making full use of his or her potential.

Organismic Abandon

Schultz discovered – as have many since – that in a state of passive concentration all activities governed by the autonomic nervous system, once believed to be out of our control, can in fact be influenced by us. This happens not by exercising any conscious act of *will* but rather by learning to abandon oneself to an ongoing *organismic* process.

This strange paradox of self-induced passivity is central to the way in which autogenic training works its wonders. It is a skill which Eastern yogis, famous for their ability to resist cold and heat, to change the rate of their heartbeat, levitate and perform many other extraordinary feats, have long practised. But until the development of *biofeedback* and autogenic training and the arrival of Eastern meditation techniques, this passive concentration largely remained a curiosity in the West, where active, logical, linear, verbal thinking has been encouraged to the detriment of practising our innate ability to simply *be*. Many experts on the psychological processes of ageing believe that it is overemphasis on the use of the conscious will in the West that makes us so prone to premature ageing and stress-based illnesses in the first place.

Get Warm and Heavy

To help his patients induce the autogenic state, Schultz worked with the sensations of heaviness and warmth. Later he added suggestions about regular heartbeat and gentle quiet breathing – two more natural physiological characteristics of relaxation – and then went on to suggestions of warmth in the belly and coolness of the forehead. These six physiologically-orientated directions – heaviness and warmth in the legs and arms, regulation of the heartbeat and breathing, abdominal warmth and cooling of the forehead – form the core of autogenic training.

A person learning autogenics goes through each of the six steps, one by one, each time he or she practises. Because of the body and mind's ability to use repetition to slip more and more rapidly into the deeply relaxed yet highly aware autogenic state, the steps become quicker to accomplish until after a few weeks or months of practising you can virtually induce a state of profound psychophysical relaxation at will. Once you have mastered the exercises they can be practised anywhere – even sitting on a bus.

Balance Life Energies

A key principle on which autogenics is based is that the body will naturally balance its life energies, biochemically and psychologically, when allowed repeatedly to enter a relaxed state. The benefits of being able to do this are virtually endless. Some of them come immediately – such as being able to counteract acute stress and fatigue, refresh yourself and clear your mind. People with high blood pressure who learn autogenics report drops in systolic (contracting) blood pressure of i.e. 11–25% or more, and 5–15% in diastolic (dilatating) pressure. Brain-wave activity also changes, inducing a better balance of right and left hemisphere that can lead to improved creativity at work and a sense of being at peace with oneself. Other benefits come more slowly over the weeks and months and years that you practise. Recoveries from bronchial asthma and a whole range of other psychosomatic disorders have been reported, as well as the elimination of self-destructive behaviour patterns and habits such as drug-taking, compulsive eating and alcoholism. As a result autogenic training is now given as standard instruction in Germany and Switzerland.

Let's Begin

Soon after you start *The 10-Day Plan* it is time to begin polishing the lens of perception and rejuvenating the psyche.

The basic autogenic exercises are simple. Taking up one of three optional postures – sitting slumped rather like a rag doll on a stool, lounging in an easy chair, or lying on your back with your arms at your side – make sure you are reasonably protected from noise and disturbances and that your clothes are loose and comfortable. It is easiest to learn autogenics lying flat on a floor or on a very firm bed. Once you have got the basic exercise under your belt you can do it just about any time, anywhere, sitting up or even very discreetly on a bus on the way to work. If you like you can record the autogenic exercises that follow on tape very slowly and play it to yourself in the beginning. I generally find, however, that it is better to learn it very simply from the words in the box below.

Go Within

Lie down on your back in bed or on the floor. Make yourself comfortable with whatever pillows or covers you need in order to do so. Close your eyes gently. Take a deep slow breath and pause for a moment. Now exhale fully and completely. Let yourself breathe slowly and naturally. Feel your body sinking back into the floor. Now repeat the following phrases to yourself slowly and silently, letting yourself savour the sensations of heaviness and warmth as you do. The first phrase is: *My left arm is heavy . . . my left arm is heavy . . .*

my left arm is heavy . . . my right arm is heavy . . . my right arm is heavy . . . my right arm is heavy . . . Let go of any tension in your arms as you say to yourself: *My left arm is heavy . . . my left arm is heavy . . . my left arm is heavy . . .* repeating each suggestion three times. Continue to breathe slowly and naturally, remembering to exhale fully. Say to yourself: *Both arms are heavy . . . both arms are heavy . . . both arms are heavy.* Let go of any tension in your arms. Then say: *Both legs are heavy . . . both legs are heavy . . . both legs are heavy . . .* As you continue to breathe slowly and naturally, say to yourself: *Arms and legs heavy . . . arms and legs heavy . . . arms and legs heavy . . . arms and legs warm . . . arms and legs warm . . . arms and legs warm . . .*

Feel It

Feel the warmth flow through to your arms and legs as you say to yourself: *Arms and legs warm . . . arms and legs warm . . . arms and legs warm . . .* Continue to breathe slowly and freely while you repeat silently to yourself: *My breathing calm and easy . . . my breathing calm and easy . . . my breathing calm and easy . . . my heartbeat calm and regular . . . my heartbeat calm and regular . . . . my heartbeat calm and regular . . .* Feel your strong, regular heartbeat as you say the words to yourself. Continue to breathe easily and say to yourself: *My solar plexus is warm... my solar plexus is warm . . . my solar plexus is warm . . .* Feel the muscles in your face relax as you say to yourself: *My forehead is cool and clear . . . my forehead is cool and clear . . . my forehead is cool and clear . . .* Enjoy the feeling of softness and calm throughout your body and say to yourself: *I am at peace . . . I am at peace . . . I am at peace . . .*

The Return

When you have finished the exercise you are ready for *the return*. It will bring you back to normal everyday consciousness: Quickly clench both fists, take a deep breath in, flex both arms up in a stretch, then breathe out slowly and completely, returning your arms with unclenched fists to your sides. Now open your eyes. Lie for a moment with your eyes open and just allow yourself to: BE HERE NOW WITH WHATEVER IS, then get up and go about your life.

When first learning autogenics, you will need to repeat each suggestion three times and the entire exercise itself needs to be repeated at three different periods each day. The best time is just before you get out of bed, just before you go to sleep, and at some other moment of the day. If there is no way you can lie down during the day you can always do the exercise sitting in a chair. If you are practising in public, for instance on a bus or at your desk in an office, draw your fists up to your chest by bending your elbows rather than bringing the whole arm above the head for the *return*.

Autogenic Triggers

Before long you will find that even the simple suggestion *my right arm is heavy* will trigger the psychophysical relaxation process in the whole body. Some people get feelings of heaviness and warmth right away. For others it can take as long as a week or two of practising three times a day for 10 or 15 minutes at a time. To everybody it comes eventually, and with it comes a profound sense of relaxation. *Cancelling* the training session occurs when you clench your hand into a fist and raise your arm straight above your head, or bend your arm and draw your fist to your shoulders, at the same time taking a deep breath and then stretching. This trains your body to return to normal consciousness right away. Meanwhile your temporary excursion into the realm of deep relaxation keeps working its magic.

Autogenic Training Made Simple

Here is an aide memoire for practice. Repeat each suggestion 3 times:

MY LEFT ARM IS HEAVY . . .

MY RIGHT ARM IS HEAVY

BOTH ARMS ARE HEAVY . . .

BOTH ARMS ARE WARM . . .

BOTH LEGS ARE HEAVY

ARMS AND LEGS HEAVY . . .

ARMS AND LEGS WARM

BREATHING IS CALM AND EASY . . . HEARTBEAT CALM AND
              REGULAR

MY SOLAR PLEXUS IS WARM . . .

MY FOREHEAD IS COOL

I AM AT PEACE

The Return:

CLENCH BOTH FISTS

TAKE A DEEP BREATH

FLEX BOTH ARMS UP IN A STRETCH

BREATHE OUT SLOWLY

RETURN ARMS

UNCLENCH FISTS

OPEN YOUR EYES

LIE FOR A MOMENT WITH EYES OPEN

BE HERE NOW WITH WHATEVER IS.

Repeat each suggestion three times, repeat the exercise three times a day.

Discharge The Blocks

Although autogenic training brings about a 'low-arousal' state similar to yoga and meditation, where parasympathetic activity dominates, it stems from exercises meant specifically to induce simple *physical* sensations, leading to a state of relaxation of a purely physical nature. The benefits which come with practising it go far beyond the physical, however. In addition to slowing the heartbeat, reducing blood pressure, regenerating and rejuvenating the body, autogenics triggers changes in the *reticular activating system* in the brain stem which can result in what are known as 'autogenic discharges'. These are a spontaneous way of de-stressing and de-ageing the body, eliminating old tensions and wiping away thought patterns that may have been inhibiting the full expression of your being.

Autogenic discharges can manifest themselves as temporary twitching of the arms or legs – much like the twitch experienced occasionally on falling into a deep sleep – during the session itself, or increased peristaltic movement – stomach grumbles – or various transient feelings of dizziness, or visual or auditory effects. These phenomena are harmless, quick to come and go, yet an important part of throwing out life-accumulated, stressful material stored in the body or psyche.

Cleansing Reactions

A few people – I myself among them – when they first begin autogenic training go through two or three weeks where a lot of old stress and emotional rubbish gets released through autogenic discharge. Old feelings of discouragement or depression or even laughter or anxiety can sometimes rise to the surface. It is important to be aware of this possibility and to be aware of what is happening if it does occur. It is only the psychic side of detox that will help renew, refresh, and rejuvenate you as old stress you have been carrying about with you comes to the surface and is permanently cleared away.

Because of this discharge phenomenon, some psychologists in the English-speaking world who teach autogenics like to work on a one-to-one basis with their students in order to help them gain perspective on what is coming up from their consciousness. In Germany and Switzerland this is not considered important. There, autogenic training is taught as a matter of course both to adults and schoolchildren with no such psychological backup. The important thing to remember is whatever surfaces is likely to be very old indeed, stuff you've been carrying around for a long time and which you are far better off without.

Three's The Charm

Begin your practice of autogenics on day 2 of *The 10-Day Plan*, while you are following the Clean Sweep Diet. It takes about 10 to 15 minutes to run through autogenics while you are learning it. Afterwards the exercises can be done much more quickly – eventually in two or three minutes if necessary. Rather like Pavlov's dog who learned to salivate simply because the bell sounded and the food appeared together so many times, the magic of autogenics depends on your continual repetition of the exercise again and again, day after day. Once the initial period of learning is completed you can then choose to practice the exercises once or twice a day whenever you like. In the process you will have gained a life-long skill that is invaluable for de-ageing the body and mind.

Within 10 days to 2 weeks of practising autogenics most people feel a steady and increasing release of creative energy and a sense that great burdens are being lifted away so that – often for the first time – they begin to feel more free to live their own life by their own values. It is rejuvenation at its very best.

The Zen of Now

There are two important aspects to making autogenic training work for you. The first is a real *acceptance* of your current circumstances or position – knowing that anything that you feel just now, whether it happens to be fear, anxiety, joy, frustration, inadequacy or environmental stress, is OK for the moment. It is only through acceptance of what is now that we open the gateways to change. The second important thing about autogenic training is self-discipline. You need to make time to do the exercises each day and to establish a routine during *The Plan* where you are practising the exercises 3 times a day. This will set up the foundation for life-long practice.

Step 8
Hydro Electrics

Water is a superb de-ager. Yet its powers are easy to overlook. For we tend to think in terms of the rare and exotic and to forget what is closest to hand. Water therapy is the oldest system of natural healing in the world. Thanks to water's chemical and bioelectrical properties and to the body's physiological and energetic responses to it, water therapy used daily is a great way to deep cleanse, energize and restore more youthful functioning to an ageing body.

Water is the universal solvent made from 3 simple molecules, 2 of hydrogen and 1 of oxygen. They are bound together to produce the most important substance on earth and in the human body. The primary substance in all of the body fluids – from digestive juices, urine, tears and sweat, to lymph and blood – water makes up at least 60% of the body. It is the medium in which most of our nutrients are found and it is involved in almost every function that you can think of from digestion, absorption of nutrients and elimination to circulation and keeping the skin plump and youthful-looking. Water also carries mineral salts and *electrolytes*. It transmits the electrical currents of life as well as all the major minerals needed to fuel metabolic processes – magnesium, for instance, as well as calcium, potassium, sodium and chloride. Internally, pure water will dissolve, transport and absorb essential nutrients as well as extracting and discarding stored wastes from the cells and tissues and eliminating them. Used externally – in the form of hot and cold baths or showers – water brings subtle yet dynamic changes in energy, hormone balance, muscle tone, circulation and nervous system functioning, as well as improved circulation. Water has an ability to transform static and stagnant conditions of mind and body into more youthful functioning. It is impossible to experience high level health, rejuvenate the body and to prevent premature ageing without an abundance of clean water.

Electrics and Therapeutics

Water is able to store and transmit heat. It will absorb more heat for a given weight than most other substances in the universe – twice as much as alcohol, ten times more than copper and thirty times more than gold. It has a density near that of the human body, which is what makes it valuable as an exercise medium for people with inflammation or injuries. Water also has the ability to change states within a very narrow temperature range. As ice it can be applied to swelling, as liquid it can be used in hot and cold applications, as steam it can be breathed to clear congested lungs or cleanse the pores of skin by herbal steaming. When you plunge your body into water in the bath hydrostatic pressure is put on the body's surface to enhance lymphatic drainage and the elimination of wastes.

Water's life-enhancing properties go way beyond the chemical. It is also useful in improving the electrical and electronic conduction mechanisms of the body. These bio-energies form the basis of many of the control mechanisms in living systems – the means by which life processes such as growth and regeneration take place. When carried out skilfully and safely hydrotherapy can bring just the kind of bio-electrical support needed to help to regenerate tissues, enhance immunity, stimulate vitality, improve circulation and enhance overall good looks and wellbeing.

Drink to Youth

Drinking plenty of water also becomes more and more important as the years pass. It is vital to prevent dry skin and constipation, both of which are associated with age. When your body is provided with enough water, circulation works better, as does lymphatic drainage, and you are less bothered by cellulite. Ironically, drinking plenty of clean water also helps eliminate water retention. When the body gets short of water it tends to hold wastes and fluids in the tissues, making skin and muscles puffy and spoiling the natural contours of face and body. Water drinking can help clear this.

How much water do you need to drink? Enough to produce 3–4 pints of urine each day – that is 1$^{1}/_{2}$ to 2 litres. Part of your daily quota can come from herb teas or natural juices made from fresh fruits and vegetables. It doesn't all have to be H$_2$O. But however you choose to take it, clean water is essential for continually detoxifying the body, keeping the intestinal tract clean.

Margin of Safety

The only trouble is, clear, clean water can be hard to find these days. Tap water is seldom totally safe. Urban water is an unnatural, highly processed, substance. It can contain many potentially hazardous chemical additives and contaminants. Here are a few of the most common:

- industrial chemicals
- pesticides
- lead
- mercury
- aluminium
- cadmium
- organic solvents
- nitrates
- chlorine
- fluoride
- xenoestrogens

Tap water tends to be heavily chlorinated in order to kill bacteria, and it is often fluoridated to prevent tooth decay. Although fluoride has been shown to reduce dental caries it is better painted on children's teeth or used in toothpastes than poured into the body. Fluoride in concentrations of as little as 8 to 20 parts per million is known to cause tissue sclerosis and contribute to arthritis. Above that level it can cause destructive alteration in the cells, especially the liver, kidneys, adrenals and reproductive organs. Many water authorities also add alkaline substances such as calcium hydroxide to water so that it does not corrode the pipes, with little thought to the effect that such chemicals will have on human health.

The major problem with chlorine and many of the other water additives is that, like pesticides, herbicides and chemical solvents, they react together with other organic chemicals to produce carcinogenic substances. For example, chlorine together with organic matter, say decaying leaves or ammonia, will form *chloramines* such as chloroform and various other *trihalomethanes* which are carcinogenic (cancer-causing). Meanwhile water pipes themselves can contribute unhealthy doses of heavy metals like lead and copper. Leave tap water for washing. Drink something better.

Spring Into Youth

Spring water is probably the best choice, provided you pick a water whose origins are well known and which has been tested and certified clean. This is where the French waters are so good. The control that is exerted over the quality of spring water in France is higher than in any other place in the world. Some of the best waters are Volvic, an exceptionally pure still water from the Auvergne mountains in Central France, and the sparkling Perrier which arrives in carbonated form from a spring in Vergèze in Southern France. Volvic is a lightly mineralized water with a vibrant quality. Vittel is another good water that wends its way through rock tunnels to pour clean and fresh from a source surrounded by 12,000 acres of conservation land in North Eastern France. It is low in sodium and rich in calcium.

Filter The Rest

As for home water filters, they vary tremendously in their effectiveness. Solid carbon filters will not remove fluoride, but are good at taking out chlorine, parasites, chemicals and some heavy metals. Reverse osmosis filters will not remove chlorine unless a carbon filter is also used, but will take out fluorides, parasites, bacteria, chemicals, as well as heavy metals and some of the basic minerals (most of which you would be better off leaving in). Distillation will remove practically everything except possibly a few toxic chemicals. But heavy-duty water purification systems can be expensive. A general rule, if your water supply is not too bad, is to use a simple portable water purification jug for the water that will be heated to cook foods, while drinking and making teas from (if you can afford it) a good French mineral water.

How Much? How Often?

Drink 2 glasses of water on awakening and another glass or two an hour to half an hour before each meal. Don't drink water with your meal or for 2 hours after a meal since it tends to dilute the digestive fluids and can interfere with the digestion and assimilation of nutrients. It may surprise you to learn this, but water is also the single most important helper in shedding excess fat and keeping it off. Drunk regularly this way it has been called a 'magic potion for weight loss'. Plenty of water taken regularly helps the body to metabolize stored fat and suppresses the appetite naturally.

Splash Splash

The deep cleansing and rejuvenating properties of water used externally are as important as its internal applications. External hydrotherapy has been used as a treatment for rejuvenation as far back as biblical times and even further than that. The Egyptians, Assyrians, Persians, Hindus and Chinese used it regularly. In Europe and in the United States external water applications were par for the course in the nineteenth century, and were used by famous natural healers and doctors like Dr J H Kellogg, and, in Germany, by Father Kneipp. These natural practitioners made continual use of water in all its forms – steam, ice, and hot and cold temperatures – in the form of full-body immersion, showers, baths, and hot and cold compresses for a myriad of healing and health-enhancing purposes. Today, external hot and cold applications are used by top athletes to enhance immunity, strengthen the body, relieve aches and pains, and keep the system in top form.

Dr Douglas Lewis, head of physical medicine at John Bastyr College Natural Health Clinic in the United States and a modern expert in hydrotherapy, outlines some of the effects of hot and cold water applications: 'Hot water produces a response that stimulates the immune system and causes white cells to migrate out of the blood vessels and into the tissue where they can clean up toxins and assist the blood in eliminating waste.' Hot showers and hot baths are therapeutically useful to relax the body. Thanks to the reflex action of hot water on the body's nervous system this kind of treatment can affect every organ and part of the system. By contrast, cold water 'discourages inflammation by means of vaso-constriction (constricting blood vessels) and by reducing the inflammatory agents, making the blood vessels less permeable. Cold water also tones muscular weakness.'

Chill Out

When cold water is applied to your body it leads to a temporary decrease in function, either locally in the area to which it is applied, or on the system as a whole, depending on how it is being used. The longer the application and the colder the water the more intense and prolonged will be this inhibitory effect.

However, your body responds quickly and intensely to cold water by creating a secondary effect that is quite the opposite. First, cold applications constrict blood vessels. Then very quickly the stimulation alters this vaso-constriction to its opposite – vaso-dilation. Putting your body into cold water at first decreases respiration. This is swiftly followed by an opening up in your breathing. And at first cold water increases the heart rate only to be followed by a rapid decrease in heart rate.

At the Koda clinic in Japan, after scrubbing and rinsing the body in the traditional Japanese way, people learn a Japanese form of hydrotherapy – to immerse themselves in alternating cold and hot tubs up to their neck. This becomes a daily practice. The hot water tubs are kept at a constant temperature of 40–41 degrees centigrade, while the cold water tubs vary between 15 and 25 degrees centigrade depending on the season. Dr Koda uses five applications alternating between cold and hot, beginning and ending with cold. By contrast, in the Western tradition of hydrotherapy, it is a principle that alternating hot and cold applications of water, repeated three to five times, always begin with a hot application and end with a cold. This is to ensure that the body never becomes chilled. Personally I find the Western way works best for athletes and those being introduced to hydrotherapy.

When I experienced my first Koda immersion therapy I felt hesitant, fearing that I would not be able to undergo the ritual without ending up looking (or sounding) like a real sissy. However, to my amazement, I discovered that once I got through the first cold application – which is always the hardest – I not only found the experience easy to handle, but actually pleasurable. Soon I was looking forward to my hydrotherapy sessions with enthusiasm.

Contrast-Hydros

When it comes to de-ageing the body, such hot and cold water applications – known as contrast-hydrotherapy – are used alternately, either as baths or showers or a combination of both, to stimulate adrenal functions, alleviate inflammation, enhance hormone production, firm skin, strengthen muscles and detox the system. The greater the contrast between the temperature of the water applied to the skin and body temperature itself, the greater the effect contrast-hydros produce.

Contrast applications of water can also be used to enhance the functions of organs in reflex relationships to the areas of the skin being treated. Applications of water over the liver, for instance, will increase its functional activity – something else that is helpful when detoxifying the system.

One of the wonderful, positive benefits that women report from contrast-hydro is a lessening of any menstrual problems such as PMS, back pains and cramps. Athletes use whole-body contrast hot and cold baths or showers after a workout to strengthen themselves, to eliminate muscular damage and pain from heavy use, and to energize the whole body. I introduced my own trainer, Welsh champion weightlifter Rhodri Thomas, to contrast-hydro a few months ago. He found that hot and cold water after each workout both protected his muscles from pain and vastly increased his strength and stamina. After a few weeks of hydrotherapy he found himself setting one new personal best after another.

Go For It

Using hydrotherapy for rejuvenation is easy, provided, of course, that you are generally healthy and not suffering from a heart condition. It is a simple matter of developing new habits. Hot water is applied to the whole body for three or four minutes in the form of a hot bath or shower, followed by thirty to sixty seconds of cold water. This procedure is repeated three times.

The application of cold water need only be long enough to make the blood vessels constrict, and this has been shown to take place in as short a period as twenty seconds. This kind of treatment helps remove wastes that have accumulated in the body and bring nutrients and oxygen to those areas as well as balancing the energies and the autonomic nervous system. Cold water intensifies the activity of the *sympathetic* nervous system while hot water intensifies *parasympathetic* activity.

Contrast-hydro makes you feel great – but it is important to start slowly, increasing the length of your exposure to hot and cold water gradually. Three minutes of hot followed by thirty to sixty seconds of cold. There are several ways you

Contrast-Hydro Protocols

- Always make sure that your body is warm before beginning any contrast-hydrotherapy. You might like to drink a cup of herb tea in the winter to this end before you start.

- See that the room that you are doing your treatment in is well heated. At no time during the treatment of hydrotherapy should the body become chilled. If you feel yourself becoming chilled, immediately stop the treatment or get into a hot bath or shower until you warm up fully.

- Don't use contrast-hydrotherapy if you have any kind of organic disease, nervous disorder, high blood pressure, are insulin-dependent diabetic, if you are very weak, or suffering from hardening of the arteries.

- Always check with your doctor before beginning any natural treatment to make sure that it is appropriate for you to use.

- Always begin with a hot application and end with a cold.

- Begin slowly with 2–3 minutes of hot application followed by 20 seconds of cold. As your body accustoms itself to contrast-hydrotherapy you can increase the time of the cold applications up to 1 minute (even up to 2–3 minutes if you are extremely fit or an athlete). But 20 seconds of cold is enough to get the effects that you need.

- After contrast-hydrotherapy dry your body well and make sure that you do not become chilled.

can do this. It can be done in the shower by taking a three-minute hot shower followed by twenty seconds to one minute of cold, repeating this three times beginning with hot and ending with cold. Alternatively, if you have a bath and shower which are separate, you can use the bath for one temperature application, the shower for the other, getting in and out of each. I particularly like doing it this way because it gives me a chance to immerse myself fully in water. During the summer make your bath cold and your showers hot. During the winter you can reverse this, making your bath hot and your shower cold.

Be Water-Wise

There are some very important rules of hydrotherapy, for like any natural treatment it has to be followed carefully and wisely both to get benefits from it and to ensure that no harm is done to the body in the process.

Sheer Exhilaration

You will probably find, as I did when I began using hot and cold applications on myself, that a plunge into cold water or a brisk cold shower is an exhilarating experience. The first effect is a slight shock on the body and then an experience of total pleasure. It is always the first cold application that is the hardest. I have come to believe that the biggest barrier to getting into cold water is a psychological one. Once this is overcome you are likely to end up really looking forward to your daily treatment.

Contrast-hydro begins on day 3 of *The 10-Day Plan*, at whatever time of the day you bathe or shower. It doesn't matter what time each day you set aside for contrast-hydrotherapy, although because contrast-hydro can be highly energizing it is often best not to do it just before bed. My favourite time is just after exercise when my body is warm and already glowing with good circulation.

If you are hesitant about getting into hydrotherapy try using a couple of buckets to start with. Fill one with hot water, one with cold, then instead of immersing the whole body as you would in a bath or shower simply plunge the feet into first the hot then the cold bucket, alternating with three minutes of hot and twenty to thirty seconds of cold. Let your body get used to the experience of contrast-hydro treatment before experimenting with baths or showers. Alternatively you can pour jugs of hot and cold water over your body while standing in the bath. If you choose to go this route make sure that the bathroom is extra well heated. You must never let your body get chilled. Then as you become accustomed to the treatment you can gradually work up to full-body treatments.

Hydro-Electric Future

It may be decades before we have a clear picture of just how hydrotherapy works its regenerative wonders on the body. We already know a lot about the physiological, biochemical and energetic benefits it can bestow. Biologists with a background in quantum mechanics are beginning to investigate the issue of how particles like electrons, atoms and molecules, behaving as biophoton energies which dictate and regulate living systems, are influenced by hydro treatments. Water treatments enhance body functions and heighten vitality, thanks to water's ability to act on the body's electromagnetic fields as well as on its physiology. But it will probably be years before we even begin to penetrate the mysteries of how water works on the body. In the meantime we have inherited a long tradition of tried and tested hydrotherapy techniques for everything from boosting athletic performance to rejuvenating the body. It would be a shame not to use it.

Step 9
Reinventing the Body

One of the most ageing influences in our lives is the force of habit. Habitual ways of thinking, moving and feeling are rather like 'grooves' into which we conveniently let ourselves fall for protection from life's surprises. Such grooves can be useful. They bring us structures of security. After all none of us can live our whole life standing on top of a cliff while the winds of change toss us about unceasingly. Yet life grooves can be stultifying too – especially when we are not fully aware of the habits of thinking, moving and feeling we have let ourselves get into. Then they limit us by exchanging the sense of free, open positive expectations about living we had when we were young into strange self-made prisons from which we seem able only to gaze through the bars at what might have been.

De-Groove Your Life

An omnipresent sense of limitation in our lives is a major characteristic of premature ageing. It not only undermines our body's movement, grace and fluidity, it spoils our capacity for joy and bliss and it also make us rigid in our thinking. It can also limit our dreams and impede our ability to turn them into reality.

An essential part of rejuvenating body and psyche is dissolving away whatever restricts ease of movement in the body, the full expression of our creativity, and the free experience of our capacity for joy. Ironically, rediscovering this kind of personal energy and freedom is almost always not so much a task of mind as of body. For it is only in opening up the body's capacity for natural movement that restrictions in our breathing, our feelings and our thinking can gradually be replaced by the adventurous, pleasurable, child-like capacity to learn and experience each moment of life to the full. With all of the mind/body techniques I have experimented with throughout the years, I have never come across a technique better at helping us do this than *Feldenkrais*. Even more wonderful, the process of learning it can be *sheer bliss*.

Russian Revolutionary

Dr Moshe Feldenkrais was a physicist, an engineer and an accomplished athlete. Born in Russia in 1919, he worked for the British Admiralty during World War II, then emigrated to Palestine where, plagued by a knee injury as a result of a sports accident, he began to search for a way of helping himself heal. The doctors he consulted had told him again and again that his leg would never function normally. So Feldenkrais began to study how the body moves. With the training of a scientist, he studied neurophysiology and neuropsychology. Before long he not only wrote a classic examination of mind/body, he was also able to throw his crutches away. His knee completely healed.

Maintaining that motor function and thought patterns are inseparable, Feldenkrais insisted that our emotions such as grief, joy, sorrow and enthusiasm are encoded within our flesh and expressed in our body postures and tensions. He then went on to develop simple *blissful* ways of helping people develop an awareness of how the body moves, feels and experiences life, in doing so aiming to come closer and closer to what he called *functional integration*. When it comes to rejuvenating body and psyche, his techniques are nothing short of revolutionary.

Feldenkrais' work has been much praised by some of the world's top artists and scientists for whom it has proved nothing short of life-changing – from Yehudi Menuhin and director Peter Brook to neuropsychologist and brain expert Dr Karl Pribram, anthropologist Margaret Mead and the late Prime Minister of Israel, David Ben-Gurion. Until his death Feldenkrais continued to perform what were amusingly called 'routine miracles', transforming the lives of both the sick and the apparently well through expanding the body's ability to move.

Joyful Balance

Functional integration is the physiological and psychological counterpart of biochemical and energetic *homeostasis* in the body. It introduces a person practising it to a centred, grounded way of living where our physical and psychic movements are open, vital and creative, rather like a young baby learning about the world around him. Practising these movements over time gradually and easily helps dissolve away emotional restrictions, and the mechanical psychic limitations of our thinking. Feldenkrais used to say: 'In a perfectly matured body which has grown without great emotional disturbances, movements tend gradually to conform to the mechanical requirements of the surrounding world. The nervous system has evolved under the influence of these laws and is fitted to them. However, in our society, we do, by the promise of great reward or intense punishment, so distort the even development of the system, that many acts become excluded or restricted. The result is that we have to provide special conditions for furthering adult maturation of many arrested functions. The majority of people have to be taught not only the special movements of our repertoire, but also to reform patterns of motions and attitudes that should never have been excluded or neglected.' This is what the fourth cornerstone of *Ten Steps to a Younger You* is all about. I call it reinventing the body.

Mindful Spontaneity

Since Feldenkrais' death his work has been continued by a number of highly trained students, each of whom has not only consolidated its power in their own teaching but also brought something of their own creativity to the way they work with the body. One of the best of these is Israeli Ruthy Alon, author of *Mindful Spontaneity*. Alon travels the world helping people experience the art of functional integration through gentle, blissful body movements that penetrate deep into a person's physical, psychic and spiritual core. Four days of working with her transformed my thinking and feeling as well as the way I related to my body and psyche. It taught me that, instead of being a constant struggle, life can be an exciting experience of unfolding and renewal from day to day. This is one of the most important secrets of youth one can ever learn. It is the secret of the innocent child – a youth secret you will never be able to put into a bottle or charge a fortune for, since, like all secrets worth knowing, it can only be discovered from within. You will only discover it for yourself through practice, for there is no way to imagine just how far reaching are the benefits of Feldenkrais without experiencing them.

Youth Process

What follows are Alon's own four processes for rejuvenating the body. They are easy to do yet powerful beyond all expectations. In my view they far surpass even the famous ancient rejuvenation rituals of Tibet and China, and they can be done by anyone at any age in just about any condition. You do each of them lying on the floor with the help of a rolled blanket or towel. The *Alon processes* are nothing like conventional exercises. They are instead gentle explorations into movement which require very little physical effort and absolutely no strain. The movements involved in each are small yet always done with awareness. In fact, awareness is the key to transformation that comes with all Feldenkrais practice. The smaller the exertion and the finer the increment or decrement that you can distinguish from each process the greater will be the mobilization of your muscles as a result of your awareness. The lighter the effort you make the faster you will learn. This is not only true in the case of practising Feldenkrais but in learning any skill. It is a truth the young child just learning to crawl or walk knows instinctively but one which we as adults usually have to re-learn.

Get Into Bliss

Begin to practise the first of the Alon processes on day 4 of *The 10-Day Plan*. On day 5 practise the second process. On day 6 work with the third process and on day 7 the fourth process. On day 8 try doing the first and second processes together. On day 9 practise the third and fourth processes. Finally on day 10 lay aside thirty to forty minutes to put all four processes together. Each previous day's body work should take you from 10 to 15 minutes. After *The Plan* has finished, you might like to practise one or more of the Alon processes three times a week. Use them too whenever you feel tense, tired or emotionally or spiritually restricted. So good are they that they may bring transformation to your life that you have never even dreamed of. They certainly have to mine.

For the first three processes you will need a single blanket or a bath towel, folded once on its width and once on its length to create a rectangle. Roll up the length of the rectangle to make a tight roller, approximately 8 cm (2½ in) in diameter and long enough to go from the top of your head to the base of your spine. If your blanket or towel is bigger than this leave some of it unrolled. For the fourth process you will also need to make a ball about the size of a fist by rolling up a thick pair of socks.

THE FIRST PROCESS

Lie flat on your back on the floor with your legs stretched out (if this is uncomfortable bend your knees or support them with a pillow). Take note of how your back feels against the floor – the places where it presses into the floor as well as the places where it does not touch the floor at all. Listen to your breathing, just let go and relax.

Now begin to flex your feet, pointing your toes up towards your head and back again towards the floor so your heels dig into the floor and your ankles bend up at a right angle. Do this slowly at first and without effort, then begin to speed the movement up rhythmically. Feel how with each flexing of the ankles the entire body is pushed towards the head, lifting the chin slightly from the throat, and how it becomes flatter on the floor. Then rest for a few moments and see if your back seems to accept the floor more easily.

Roller Play

Now you are ready for the roller. Take your roller and lie so that your right hip and right shoulder are resting along its length and your left hip and shoulder are leaning on the floor. Make sure that the right half of your pelvis and your right shoulder-blade are resting fully on the roller. Extend your legs to their full length. Take a moment to get used to the feeling of lying on something that is not perfectly horizontal.

Now bend your knees so that your feet are flat on the floor. Moving both your knees slowly over to the right and keeping your right elbow on the floor for support, allow the left hip to lift from the floor until it is level with the roller. Gently let it find the floor again. Repeat this movement, each time taking the knees to the right and letting your hip lift gently while allowing the left shoulder to rise up too. Remember to breathe easily throughout the movement and to do everything without effort. Enjoy the feeling, don't *work* at it.

Rocking Play

Extend your legs out straight again and relax. Still with your right hip on the roller, flex your ankles again, repeating the oscillating movement with your feet. Find a rhythm that feels comfortable and enjoy it. Then rest for a few moments.

Repeat the whole movement again, but this time as you come back down to the floor change the angle of your right foot. Keep the ball of the foot steady on the floor but move the heel. Continue lifting the left side of your body, each time exploring another way of placing your foot on the floor. Once you feel you have experimented enough with the ball of your foot in one place, move the foot altogether – further away from your pelvis, to the right or to the left – and go through the procedure of moving the angle of the heel again.

Discover where your foot feels the most comfortable for you and rest there for a moment.

Inhibit For Freedom

Now extend the legs and oscillate your feet again. Still moving your feet, put your left hand under your head for support, place your right hand over your chin, resting your arm and elbow on the chest, and open your mouth slightly. This inhibits the movement of the neck, making it a continuation of the spine, so that when your body moves from side to side your neck and head move with it. Lie still and rest for a moment.

Now bend your knees again, keeping your feet on the floor. Tilt both knees to the right and begin to slide the instep of your left foot along the floor, elongating the leg, brushing the floor all the way down until the knee is straight. Then tilt the right knee over towards the left, turning your body over to the left as you do so. Bring your knees back up together and repeat the movement several times, feeling how the pelvis is being lifted through a flowing movement of the legs as if you are swimming. Rest.

Extend your legs out straight, inhibit your neck again by putting your right hand over your chin and supporting your head with the left, and oscillate your feet again. Rest.

Check the Changes

When you are ready, very slowly roll a little to the left and begin to release the roller from under you as gently as you can. Lie flat on your back on the floor and notice how your back rests against the floor differently.

Gently roll onto your side, slowly sit up and then stand. Be aware of how your body feels now that you are upright. Begin to walk and see if you are walking any differently.

Finally repeat the whole exercise for the other side of your body, lying with your left hip and shoulder on the roller and moving the right side.

THE SECOND PROCESS

Taking your roller, lie on it so that it is placed straight down your spine from the top of your head to your tailbone. Lay your arms on the floor, palms downwards, slightly away from the body and rest here for a moment. Oscillate your feet again, flexing them alternately. Enjoy the waves of movement from the tips of your feet to the top of your head. This mimics the movement of walking, but in this position your vertebrae are supported. Rest for a moment.

Bend your knees so that your feet are flat on the floor and make sure that your elbows are free enough to move, supporting your arms with the heels of your hands.

Very gently lower your right hip towards the floor. Allow the rest of your body to accommodate the movement so that your left elbow moves towards the left hip, your right elbow bends, the left hip lifts and your head turns towards the left. If this is uncomfortable then don't slide the hip all the way to the floor. Rest.

Gently come back to the centre and rest, then repeat that same movement several times. Each time you come back to lie straight on the roller, allow your right foot to push against the floor slightly to support your back.

Extend your legs for a while, then bring them back up again and work with sliding your left hip onto the floor.

When you have worked on both sides extend your legs and oscillate your feet. Inhibit your neck and gently flex your feet again. Rest.

Row Easy

Bend your knees once more, interlace your fingers and place them flat on the centre of your chest. Make a rowing movement: taking the right elbow down towards the floor, extend it to the right, raise it towards the ceiling, then come back to the centre. Repeat this movement to the left, taking the left elbow towards the floor, extending to the left, raising towards the ceiling, and bringing it back to the centre, all gently. Row with the elbow of each arm alternately, keeping the palms on the chest. Enjoy the gentle rhythm throughout your body. When you have had enough, let your legs slide down and take a good rest. Oscillate your feet again, then let go of everything and rest.

Bend your knees and put them to one side so that you can roll away from the roller. Push the roller away to the side and lie flat on the floor again. Take a few moments to adjust to the new position (some people feel that the roller is still there) then come slowly to a standing position.

THE THIRD PROCESS

Place your roller on the floor and lie so that you make a T shape with the roller supporting the gap in your neck that usually would not touch the floor. Set the roller so that it fills the entire gap from your shoulders to your skull. Your face is now parallel to the ceiling and the back of your head can be slightly lifted from the floor. Use your common sense in adjusting the roller until you are really comfortable.

Rest for a while in this position; if it is uncomfortable support your head with a cushion as well. With your legs extended, oscillate your feet and enjoy the sensation along your spine and up into your neck. Rest.

Bend your right knee, place your right hand on your forehead and allow yourself to rock your head very gently to the left and back to the centre. Very gently allow the heel of the hand to roll the head to the left and the fingers to pull the head back again. Put your right hand back on the floor and roll the head to the right and back to the centre using your left hand.

Thread Your Hair

Comb your hair with both hands from the forehead to the back of the head. Allow your fingers to push through the hair and grab the hair where the head meets the floor. Bring your elbows as close together as you can and direct them towards your chest, lifting the head very slightly from the floor. Bring your head back to the floor and see how the vertebrae yield to the shape of the roller and spread out into a uniform arch. Repeat this movement several times. Each time you lift your head imagine that someone is holding your elbows so that your head and neck feel suspended. Enjoy it. Rest.

Extend your legs and oscillate your feet. Rest.

Bend your knees and extend your arms in front of you towards the ceiling. Stretch up further with your right arm and bend the left elbow slightly. Bend the right elbow slightly and stretch up with the left hand. Repeat this movement several times as if you are walking on the ceiling. As you stretch your arm up, keep the palm pointing towards the feet, as you bend your elbow turn the palm slowly towards the face. When you feel you have done enough, rest.

Repeat the movement, this time raising your hips. As you stretch up with your right hand, raise the right hip and move slightly over to the left, allowing the left foot to support you. When you stretch with the left hand, raise the left hip, move slightly to the right and rest your weight on your right foot.

In this way you are walking with both your hands and your feet, allowing the roller to massage your neck.

At the Head of Freedom

Still using this walking motion, begin to change your place on the roller, supporting the vertebrae at the base of your neck to work your shoulders. Allow your head to roll from side to side with the movement so that when the right arm is stretched and the right hip is lifted, the head has rolled to the left. Enjoy the massage this gives to the whole of your upper back. Keep repeating the movement, concentrating on any areas you feel need more work, then rest.

Extend your legs and oscillate your feet again. Inhibit the neck and flex your feet again. Now gently roll on your side with your knees bent. Move the roller away and lie flat on the floor. Notice how your back feels now against the floor. When you are ready slowly stand up and see what kind of back you have now. Walk around a little. Would you say that now your back is carrying around a little less 'history' than before?

THE FOURTH PROCESS

Now you will need your thick socks made into a ball to go beneath your pelvis. Lie on your back, bend your knees so that your feet are flat on the floor and feel how your pelvis is making contact with the floor. Notice where the pressure is greatest and if you feel your pelvis is symmetrical.

Imagine you are lying with your pelvis on the face of a clock so that 12 o'clock is at your tail bone, 6 o'clock is at your waistline where the spine meets the pelvis, 3 o'clock is at the right hip, and 9 o'clock is at the left hip. Take your ball made from a pair of thick socks and place it to support your sacrum between your tail bone and your waist – the centre of the clock face. Rest here. If the ball feels too big to be comfortable then make it smaller.

Press your tail bone down towards the floor so that your waistline comes off the ground. Come back to your original position and repeat the movement, rocking your pelvis towards 12 o'clock and coming back again.

Keeping the tail bone on the floor, begin to walk from one foot to the other, just lift one foot from the floor and put it down again as you lift the other. Come back to your original position and rest.

Easy Circles

Place one hand at the small of your back with the palm on the floor. Gently press your waistline onto the floor at 6 o'clock and feel with your hand how you increase the pressure there. Try to do this without tightening the stomach – remember that any change in the back does not have to be paid for by the stomach.

Keeping the pressure at 6 o'clock walk from one foot to the other. Come back to the centre and rest.

Bring your right hand to support your right hip by placing it palm down under the right buttock. Begin to shift the pressure onto your right hip, at 3 o'clock. Feel the pressure on your hand, and move back to the centre.

Repeat this several times. Press down onto 3 o'clock and walk from one foot to the other again. Repeat this movement with your left hip, at 9 o'clock, moving to the centre and back again and finally walking with your left hip pressed to the floor. Come back to the centre and rest.

Gently remove the pair of socks and let your pelvis rest on

the floor. Keep your knees bent and see how the floor feels against your pelvis. Extend your legs and rest.

Be Clockwise

When you are ready bend your knees again and put the ball back at the centre of your clock. This time shift the pressure to 12 o'clock, the tail bone, and from there go a quarter of the circle to 3 o'clock. Come back to 12 o'clock and go a quarter of the circle to 9 o'clock on the left. Come back to 12 o'clock. Repeat this movement with the lower back several times. Let the whole of your body be involved in this movement, allow your head to do what it wants to do, allow even your shoulders to join in. Allow the weight to shift slightly from foot to foot as you do this exercise, not quite walking, but allowing the feet to react to the movement in your lower back. Come back to the centre and rest.

Next, press 6 o'clock to the floor, allowing your lower back to move a little closer to the ground. From here go a quarter of the circle to 3 o'clock on the right, come back to 6 o'clock whilst lifting your tail bone so that your waist line can have more contact with the floor, then a quarter of the circle to the left, and come back to 6 o'clock. Repeat this movement several times and rest.

Now you can take in the whole circle of the clock face. Starting at 12 o'clock begin to gradually shift the pressure around the clock, clockwise, until every digit of the clock has made contact with the floor. When you are ready change direction and go anti-clockwise all the way around again. Allow the rest of your body to move in sympathy.

Once more move in a clockwise direction, but this time inhibit your neck – one hand over your chin, your arm resting on your chest, the other hand supporting the back of the head. Move in an anti-clockwise direction once again, then rest.

Sock Rocks

Remove the ball of socks and feel how your pelvis accepts the ground now. Rest here and when you are ready put the ball of socks back in the centre of the clock and carry out the movement clockwise and anti-clockwise a few more times.

Slowly begin to let go of the full circular movement and begin to walk from one foot to the other, allowing your pelvis to create a half circle, from 12 o'clock to 3 o'clock, to 12 o'clock to 9 o'clock and so on, as you move your feet.

When you are ready step slightly to the right with both feet as you walk. Stay in this position for a moment then go back to moving your pelvis around the clock. Return to walking with your feet and completing a half circle. Come back to the centre. Repeat the movement to the left.

Finally, repeat the whole sequence by moving from 6 o'clock to 3 o'clock, from 3 o'clock to 6 o'clock and from 6 o'clock to 9 o'clock, working on the upper half of the clock face. Come back to the centre and rest.

Remove the pair of socks and notice how the floor feels. Gently slide your legs down, one then the other, brushing your feet along the floor until your legs are straight. Rest.

Slowly find your way to a standing position and walk around. Take time to get used to your new way of moving and the new freedom of your whole being.

Practice Makes Blissful

Simple as they are, these four processes are life-changing: but, like anything else, they need to be practised to work their wonders. Practising an Alon process for 10–20 minutes a couple of times a week after *The 10-Day Plan* is finished will continue to reinvent your body and psyche year after year. After a while they become like old friends whom you can return to for comfort, for pleasure and for transformation. They work especially well when your body aches with fatigue or after exercise. Bringing you greater freedom of movement and increased capacity for physical and emotional joy, all the while they continue re-educating your body and psyche to wider horizons and rejuvenating your whole being.

THE 10-DAY REJUVENATION PLAN CHECKLIST

Here's what it looks like in practice.

Day One:
Begin Clean Sweep Diet and organize your foods for the week. Be sure to drink 2 glasses of water on awakening and the rest of your quota throughout the day, every day from now on.

Day Two:
Start autogenic training and practise it for 5 to 10 minutes three times a day until Clean Sweep is finished, then cut down to twice or once a day.

Day Three:
Add contrast-hydros today and from now on practise them once a day from Day 3 onwards whenever you bathe or shower.

Day Four:
Begin Feldenkrais techniques today exploring Ruthy Alon's Process One just once today. You will need 10–20 minutes for this. It can be done at any time of the day and works well just before or after an autogenic session.

Day Five:
Today, leave Alon Process One for the moment and explore Process Two. Continue with autogenics and contrast-hydros as well as the diet.

Day Six:

Now move on to Alon Process Three.

Day Seven:

Now move ahead to the Fourth Process. Take stock of how you are getting on with autogenics. Are you beginning to experience feelings of heaviness and warmth?

Day Eight:

Continue with autogenics and contrast-hydros as usual. Practise Alon Process One again, and move on to Process Two.

Day Nine:

Today practise Alon Process Three, then move on to Process Four along with your other practises.

Day Ten:

Now, draw together all the practices. Put aside half an hour or more today to go through all the Alon Processes beginning with One and going on smoothly to the others in order. Check your autogenic practice. How is it coming along? Is this something you would like to continue with after Clean Sweep is finished but perhaps only once or twice a day? What about the contrast-hydros? Congratulate yourself. You have carried out a programme that requires discipline and dedication. At the same time forgive yourself for any way in which you have not completely fulfilled your intentions. None of us is perfect. Sit down with a piece of paper and pencil and make some plans for tomorrow and next week and maybe even next month. Decide what from Clean Sweep you want to keep. Look at what permanent changes you want to make.

Step 10
Youth Strategies for Life

*T*he *10-Day Plan* plunges you deep into the processes of rejuvenation so you begin to taste its sweetness. Now it is time to look at a de-ageing lifestyle that can carry on the process.

Life at the end of the millennium is not easy. We are exposed to toxic chemicals, heavy metals, electromagnetism and noise pollution every day of our lives. If we live in an urban environment, the chances are that we live stressed lives – often without as much support from our families and communities as we would like. The techniques you have learned during the past ten days will be powerful allies for survival in the twenty-first century. If you carry on practising them you will continue to enhance your physical and psychological integration as well as furthering the important de-ageing process that helps protect you from degenerative diseases. You can continue looking and feeling great as the years pass. But there are other ways in which we also need to look after ourselves.

Dump The Drugs

One of the major actions you can take to protect yourself from premature ageing in the long term is to stay away from drugs. Many drugs interfere with mineral absorption and undermine metabolic functions. Acid drugs bind calcium and other minerals like zinc and magnesium, making them unavailable for your body to use in those important enzymes that fuel energy and cell reproduction. Without first-rate enzyme activity no-one can function optimally. Diuretics or 'water pills' – given to eliminate water retention – trigger the kidneys to excrete potassium and can lead to potassium deficiency. Although many doctors now give extra potassium with diuretic drugs, diuretics also increase the body's output of zinc, magnesium and other minerals (something of which most doctors are still unaware) so that deficiencies in these elements develop. Antibiotics disturb the balance of intestinal flora, creating *dysbiosis*. The helpful bacteria needed for the production of certain important B-complex vitamins, vitamin K, and for protection against cancer are destroyed along with the bad-guy bacteria that antibiotics are trying to kill off in the body. Most laxatives can also be very damaging to the system. Many contain mineral oils which bind the fat-soluble vitamins K, E, D and A, leaching them from the tissues. Even when drugs are prescribed by your doctor, keep a close watch on what you are taking. It's a good idea to buy a book on drugs and their interactions so you keep well informed about anything it is suggested you take into your body.

Reproductive Distortions

In our modern industrialized world it is all too easy for our reproductive biochemistry to become distorted and youthful functioning to be undermined as a result. In the past fifty years male sperm count in the Western world has fallen by almost half. Meanwhile, women are experiencing the rise of a whole new – as yet largely unrecognised – phenomenon known as *oestrogen dominance*. Oestrogen dominance is where a woman's oestrogen levels far outweigh progesterone in her body, making her prone to cancer, menstrual miseries and menopausal agonies.

There are two classes of major reproductive hormones in a woman's body – the oestrogens (which are commonly lumped together and called 'oestrogen') and progesterone. When these two are in good balance a woman's health thrives. She remains free of PMS and other menstrual troubles. She also remains fertile and able to hold a foetus to full term; and menopause becomes a simple transition instead of a passage riddled with suffering. And she is protected from fibroids, endometriosis and osteoporosis. She is also likely to remain emotionally balanced and free of excessive anxiety or depression. When oestrogen and progesterone are not in balance, a woman's body becomes oestrogen dominant and she can come a cropper.

Watch Out For Xenoestrogens

Oestrogen dominance in women and the drop in sperm count in men have come about for several reasons, the two major ones being the widespread use of oestrogen-based oral contraceptives and the exponential spread of chemicals in our environment. Called *xenoestrogens* – oestrogen mimics – these unfriendly substances are taken up by the oestrogen receptor sites in our bodies and promptly throw spanners in the works. They include the petro-chemical derivatives we take in as herbicides and pesticides which have been sprayed on our foods, the plastic cups we drink our tea from as well as the oestrogens that come through in drinking water recycled from our rivers. Oestrogens from the Pill and HRT are excreted in a woman's urine. They can end up back in our water supply, as hormones are not removed by standard water purification treatments. To stay vital each of us needs to be aware of the potential dangers of the 'sea of oestrogens' in which we are now living.

The proliferation of xenoestrogens in our environment needs to be stopped. It is making men less fertile and women more prone to breast and womb cancer, fibroid tumours, endometriosis, osteoporosis and infertility, not to mention a long list of emotional and mental imbalances. Yet much of the medical profession, as well as the general public, still remains largely unaware of the damage these dangerous chemicals are effecting on our lives and the lives of animals. As a result oestrogens continue to be prescribed heavily as part of HRT – not only to the handful of women who around the time of menopause may need a little extra oestrogen temporarily – but to thousands of others whose lives would be far better off without it.

Go For Protection

You can help protect yourself from excess chemical oestrogens by not microwaving foods in plastic containers, by avoiding birth control pills and HRT, by not drinking from plastic cups, by ensuring that you eat foods grown without chemical fertilizers, herbicides and pesticides, and by including in your diet foods rich in *phytosterols*. These weak, hormone-like compounds, derived from plants, can help protect us by locking into oestrogen-receptor sites in the body and preventing the much stronger xenoestrogens from gaining purchase in our bodies. Foods with good levels of phytosterols include soy-based products like tofu, yams, peas, papayas, bananas, cucumbers, raw nuts, bee pollen, sprouted seeds and grains (such as alfalfa sprouts) plus the herbs licorice root, red clover, sage, sarsaparilla and sassafras. Following Clean Sweep Diet regularly a couple of times a year can also help detox the system and keep these poisonous chemicals from building up in the long term.

Watch for Deficiencies

Much free radical damage and many of the problems associated with ageing – from depression and insomnia to fatigue, poor eyesight or hearing, fragile bones, stiffness, and aches and pains – are the result of poor diet and the resulting nutritional deficiencies. Nutritional deficiencies are now widespread in the developed countries of the Western world. This is not because we don't have enough to eat, but because we have disturbed the healthy balance of minerals and other nutrients in natural foods thanks to chemically based agriculture and excessive food processing. A number of large-scale research projects carried out in the past five years show that someone living on the typical diet of convenience foods over the years becomes deficient in vitamins and minerals. As we get older the most common deficiencies are in potassium, zinc, chromium, iron, copper, calcium, magnesium, vitamin A, vitamin B_1, vitamin B_2, vitamin B_6, vitamin B_{12}, folic acid and vitamin C, as well as in protein and fibre. Fibre from fresh vegetables, grains and pulses becomes particularly important as we get older. Unless the colon functions properly so that wastes are eliminated efficiently, constipation becomes a problem, so that the build-up of toxicity in the body increases the rate at which ageing occurs.

A national food survey carried out recently in Great Britain showed that the average person is 'grossly deficient' in six out of eight vitamins and minerals. And the problem seems to be growing worse and worse as convenience food eaters become increasingly depleted in folic acid, zinc, vitamin B_6, vitamin C and iron. The survey showed that the average person in Britain gets only 51% of the European recommended daily allowance of zinc, and only 71% of that for iron. Similarly 40% of the people studied received less than the recommended daily allowance for calcium.

Nutritional deficiencies produce premature degeneration. Avoid them by avoiding processed foods as much as you can, using sea vegetables in your cooking and salads and adding more of the green superfoods to your diet.

Choose Fats Carefully

Most of the fats that we eat today have been severely tampered with. Instead of being in a chemical form which your body can make use of (the *cis* form) to build cell walls and make hormones and prostaglandins – all of which are essential to de-age the body – we are eating *trans fatty acids*. These 'junk fats' found in margarines, golden vegetable oils and all of the convenience foods that we devour – from ready-made meals we pop into the microwave to mayonnaise, breads and spreads – can undermine health. Trans fatty acids make up a large proportion of the fats used in making biscuits, sweets, imitation cheeses, margarines, pastries, potato crisps, puddings, and nearly all the packaged and processed food products you find on supermarket shelves. Experts in fat metabolism now blame our ever-increasing consumption of trans fatty acids and our ever decreasing consumption of essential fatty acids in no small part for premature ageing and the growth of degenerative diseases including heart attacks and cancer. About the best oil you can use for salads and wok frying is extra virgin cold-pressed olive oil. It is a mono-unsaturate and much more stable for wok frying foods and making salad dressings. Canola oil is also good but harder to find.

Gut Feelings

Another major reason why vitamin, mineral and protein deficiencies tend to occur as we get older is that poor eating over many years often results in the diminishing of a person's ability to digest and assimilate nutrients from their food.

This is why, for some people, even eating a good diet is not enough to supply the nutrients needed. Deficiencies in minerals, a low level of hydrochloric acid in the stomach (essential for the absorption of nutrients) or low levels of digestive enzymes are common causes of the poor assimilation that produces nutritional deficiencies.

Food allergies and other allergies are also commonly linked with low levels of hydrochloric acid in the gut. This can be corrected gradually, by eating a nutrient-rich/calorie-poor diet of wholesome foods and by learning to manage daily stress using a technique like autogenics. Many experts in natural medicine also suggest drinking the juice of half a lemon squeezed into water or taking a teaspoon of cider vinegar in a glass of warm water twenty to thirty minutes before meals to enhance digestion. Useful, too, are good quality supplements of the major digestive enzymes such as *bromelin*, extracted from pineapples, and *papain*, from papayas. Papain is soothing to the stomach and very gentle. It helps in protein digestion. Bromelin is an anti-inflammatory enzyme which reduces tissue irritation. The pancreas secretes other enzymes important to digestion such as the *lipases*, *amylases* and *proteases*. For anyone who experiences problems with digestion a good natural combination of digestive enzymes can be a great adjunct to de-ageing. One or two capsules with a main meal will usually do the trick. But make sure you choose only the best as there are many poor imitations on the market (see Resources, p. 183).

Sleep A Lot

Sleep is a great anti-oxidant and rejuvenator to which few people pay enough attention. Even age researchers are only beginning to be aware of what a potent effect good sleep can have on de-ageing the body. Sleep is every bit as essential as quality food, good regular exercise and a healthy environment in rejuvenating the body.

In recent years *melatonin*, the hormone secreted primarily by the pineal gland during the night hours in the absence of light, has been shown to play a major role in controlling the body's circadian rhythms and awareness of time. It has also drawn much attention from age researchers. Melatonin in supplement form can be used to great advantage wherever time awareness has been distorted, such as when crossing time zones or for people who suffer from insomnia. There are many indications that melatonin also offers powerful protection against the body's most destructive free radical – the *hydroxyl* radical. Sadly, melatonin has been taken off the market in Canada and Britain – amidst a great deal of hooha about it being 'dangerous' – despite the fact that it is a natural hormone. Having looked in depth at the whole issue of melatonin I am convinced that used wisely and appropriately it is an extremely useful supplement and that there is nothing dangerous about it. Hopefully one day soon it will reappear. It is still widely available in the United States and most other countries.

New Radical Quencher

Meanwhile, when it comes to continual de-ageing of the body, the improvement witnessed in people's lives through melatonin supplementation has made researchers ask an important question: Why would the body only secrete a substance like melatonin – a powerful free radical quencher – at night and not during the day? One of the world's experts on the anti-oxidant effects of melatonin, Dr Russell Reiter, believes that from a biological point of view the primary purpose of sleep may be to create a situation in which the free radicals which we generate during the day (when our exposure to free radical damage is the highest) can be mopped up at night. And it is during the hours of darkness that the body's natural melatonin levels rise. This could well be the reason why many hard-to-treat problems such as food allergies, multiple sclerosis and ME are often tremendously improved by getting a good night's sleep. Researchers investigating sleep have also discovered that when the body accumulates high levels of free radicals, a sense of sleepiness tends to set in. Whenever this happens it is a good idea to give in to it and have a nap. At night, if you have difficulty sleeping, consider using a natural botanical such as passiflora or valerian to help. Everyone's need for sleep is different and while it is true that many of us sleep less as we get older, regular restorative slumber is important for de-ageing the body. Enjoy it.

Eat Yourself Young

Now we come to the crux of de-ageing: light eating on nutrient-rich/calorie-poor fare. After Clean Sweep how do you begin to make permanent changes in your eating habits? The answer is gradually and with enormous patience towards yourself. You can do it by continuing some of the practices that make up Clean Sweep, like replacing the usual breakfast of processed foods, tea or coffee with a green drink or energy shake, and by making one meal a day a gorgeous raw salad based on a delicious combination of crunchy vegetables with a light grain dish – brown rice, kasha, polenta, or barley pilaff – then having a light soup or protein-based sandwich for the other meal.

Some people prefer to eat only one meal a day, taking green drinks and energy shakes at the other two meal times. I like this approach and find it works particularly well for me especially because I do a lot of travelling. I carry my powdered mixed green supplement with me, put a tablespoon of it into a glass of spring water or juice in a shaker and I have an instant non-meal meal. When I have access to a blender I will mix green leaves from the greengrocer, garden or fields, with a whole banana, an apple or other fruit in spring water or soya milk to make a quick energy shake. Still other people prefer a light eating approach which keeps to the conventional three-meals-a-day yet reduces the quantities of foods at each meal.

The Koda approach to long-term eating concentrates the majority of calories at lunch and dinner and is, of course, geared to Japanese foods and eating traditions. It virtually does away with breakfast, uses no meat and – unless you choose to eat fish – is basically vegan since it uses no dairy products and no eggs. Koda emphasizes raw vegetables in his juices which are made not in a juice extractor but by putting whole fresh vegetables and green leaves into fresh water in a powerful blender and then pulverising them. Koda's diet can

---

KODA'S LIGHT EATING

Breakfast

a green drink made from fresh vegetables and green leaves

Lunch

a whole grain dish such as 75 g (3 oz) of brown rice, together with a protein food such as 200 g (7 oz) of tofu, some creamed sesame and some powdered kelp or other seaweed

Dinner

another glass of vegetable juice made from whole vegetables plus green leaves before dinner, then a different grain dish together with vegetables, seaweed, pulses or small fish, plus 10 g (1/2 oz) of sesame seeds

Drink 1 to 1 1/2 litres (3 to 4 pints) of water and/or persimmon leaf tea a day. Never drink at meal times or for three hours afterwards.

Total: approximately 1,200 calories a day

be adapted to our own Western eating style relatively easily, by using grain dishes, porridge, rye bread, and with vegetables, seaweeds and pulses.

American Style

Roy Walford prefers to spread the calories out a bit. He suggests a day's fare that contains 1,800–2,400 calories a day looks something like this:

WALFORD'S NUTRIENT-RICH/ CALORIE-POOR FARE

Breakfast

a baked apple with cottage cheese *or*
3/4 cup of fat-free dry cereal with 1 cup low-fat milk and a banana, coffee or tea

Lunch

2 slices of whole wheat bread with 85 g (3 oz) of turkey breast, tomato, lettuce and mustard, plus a sliced egg white *or*
1 pitta sandwich with 1/3 cup low-fat hummus, tomato and lettuce
1 cup tomato juice
1/2 cup grapes

Dinner

85 g (3 oz) of broiled (grilled) salmon, swordfish or halibut
1/2 baked potato topped with low-fat garlic sauce *or*
85 g (3 oz) broiled (grilled) chicken breast
1 cup whole wheat pasta with low-fat pesto sauce
1/2 carrot and 2 stalks broccoli, steamed

Plus a snack of 1/2 peach with 1/2 cup of low-fat yoghurt or one of the delicious low calorie, low-fat desserts from his excellent books (see Further Reading, p. 187)

Both Koda and Walford make good use of nutrient-rich/ calorie-poor foods in their menus. These include: nori seaweed, shiitake mushrooms, soybeans or soybean products such as tofu, kombu, and whole grains as well as fresh vegetables.

The advantage of the Walford approach is that it is very much geared to our Western tastes and is therefore perhaps easier to make the change-over to it. The advantage of the Koda approach is that it is far simpler to carry out and more in keeping with traditions of natural health and healing with its emphasis on fresh foods. Because it does not include a snack and because most of the calories are concentrated in two meals a day rather than three, for some, including me, it may be easier to carry out. It is often easier to eat one or two larger meals a day than three smaller ones which are just about equal in size. The important thing to remember is that learning to eat light on nutrient-rich foods is a spiritual as well as a physical practice. It needs to be approached with infinite patience towards yourself and gentle perseverance. In my experience it is always a case of taking three steps forward and two backward until gradually, slowly but inexorably, our habits become re-educated and eating light becomes a simple matter.

Natural Appetite Control

What happens when you go on to light eating, in whichever way works best for you, is you find that hunger lessens. This is especially true after ten days of detoxing the system on Clean Sweep. Light eating takes the pressure off the digestive system since many foods are eaten raw. Raw foods are full of enzymes which enhance the body's ability to digest foods, and in light eating one is never eating to excess. This protects the body from over-production of free radicals and releases life energy for day-to-day activities.

Animal research and clinical experience with human beings now show what eating light can do for you:

Benefits of Light Eating

- rejuvenate the body in medically measurable ways
- decrease susceptibility to damage from radiation in the environment
- continually detoxify the body, decreasing susceptibility to damage by chemical poisons
- increase your lifespan
- improve the quality of your life physically, mentally and spiritually
- help protect from damage to the reproductive system as a result of xenoestrogen exposure
- help prevent cancer
- enhance immune functions and help protect from allergies and auto-immune disorders
- help protect from osteoporosis
- lower high blood pressure
- create greater mental clarity and emotional balance
- improve the texture and look of skin, nails and hair
- eliminate chronic fatigue and increase stamina
- practice benevolence towards all living things and the planet
- save money

Will you lose weight by eating light? Of course you will. Yet Roy Walford says the drop in intake on nutrient-rich/calorie-poor eating should lead to a weight loss no greater than about 10 per cent for women and 18 per cent for men over the first six-month period. He also points out that a 20% restriction in the calories you are taking in means that you are still getting 80% of what you would have been getting before. Any greater restriction than this could have dangerous adverse side effects.

Both Koda and Walford insist that even a 20% restriction is only safe if you are especially careful about the quality of the food you are eating. This is why light eating bears no resemblance to the kind of calorie restriction imposed by slimming diets. The weight loss which occurs is a natural and *incidental* part of your body restoring normality when provided with nutrient-rich fare. If you are menstruating and notice menstrual irregularities develop you may be losing too much weight too fast. Check your diet. It must provide the very best nutritional value. Should you discover you have to sleep a lot more than usual or become fatigued or light-headed, slow down. You are probably losing too much weight too quickly.

Never shed more than 20 to 25% (as an absolute maximum) of your initial weight. If you were very lean to begin with this would be far too much. Consult your doctor about how great a weight loss is appropriate for you. Choose a doctor who is informed about nutrition and interested in working with you to achieve a higher level of wellbeing. Your doctor can be helpful in other ways, too. Before you begin a long-term programme of light eating he or she can measure your fasting blood sugar level, total white cell count, cholesterol, blood pressure and other physiological parameters which act as biomarkers of age so that together you can keep a record of how they have improved over the months.

Here are some general guidelines when choosing your foods:

Light Eating on Nutrient-Rich Foods

Foods to Use	Foods to Avoid
organic foods whenever possible	all foods containing chemical additives and colourings such as aspartame, monosodium glutamate, MSG, tartrazine, etc
1 1/2–2 litres (3–4 pints) of good spring water or filtered water each day	sodas, squashes, colas – even the sugarless diet versions
herb teas such as mint, camomile, lemon grass, ginger, persimmon leaf and vervain, green tea	coffee, tea, decaffeinated coffee
raw fruits and vegetables	packaged and/or processed fruit and fruit juices
green vegetables and super green foods like spirulina, chlorella, the green cereal grasses and Pure Synergy	corn starch, corn syrup, maize and anything containing them
free-range eggs, lamb, turkey, chicken, tuna and cold water fish such as sardines, mackerel, salmon and halibut, if you feel you need to eat flesh products	meats like beef, pork and veal
porridge made from steel-cut whole oats or chopped oat groats, whole grain dishes like polenta, kasha, brown rice, bulgar wheat	processed breakfast cereals
100% whole grain bread (read labels carefully)	anything made from refined grains and white flour including pasta, biscuits, breads and cereals
foods rich in phyto-hormones such as soya products – tofu, soya cheese, soya milk, tamari – yams, peas, bananas, bee pollen, sprouted seeds and grains	dairy products like milk, cheese, ice cream and yoghurt
sea salt, garlic, ginger, cinnamon, cilantro, parsley, sage, rosemary, thyme, cayenne, oregano, cumin, cayenne	artificial sweeteners, artificial creamers and dessert toppings

Foods to Use	Foods to Avoid
pulses such as red lentils, lentils, split peas, kidney beans, soya beans, chickpeas	sugar and anything that contains it including jams, sweets, syrups, chocolate, biscuits and sweet desserts
fresh sesame, sunflower, pumpkin seeds, almonds, fresh nuts (not peanuts)	peanuts and salted, roasted nuts
extra virgin olive oil, canola oil	processed vegetable oils, margarines and anything containing hydrogenated fats
organic miso and other natural fermented foods	any foods or drinks – even those on the 'To Use' list – to which you suspect you might be sensitive or allergic: avoid anything containing them

How About Supplements?

One of the most common concerns is whether or not on light eating you need to take multiple vitamin and mineral supplements. It is a hard one to answer. Walford believes so. He recommends supplements of beta-carotene, Vitamins E, C, and selenium together with good multivitamin/multimineral capsules. Koda finds that with careful choice of foods and great attention to how they are prepared, supplements are not generally necessary. Every person is a biochemical individual so only the roughest guidelines about nutritional supplements can be useful. Specific nutritional programmes are best devised with the help of a skilled nutritional advisor. Unless there is a particular individual need for high levels of a specific nutrient or an obvious deficiency in it, I have come to believe that the best nutritional supplements available for most people are the neutraceuticals and superfoods like spirulina, chlorella, green barley and wheat grass, shiitake and maitake mushrooms and combinations of them such as Pure Synergy. They contain complexes of important vitamins, minerals and trace elements plus other anti-ageing plant factors in a form that is balanced and easily assimilated by the body. What matters most is what you eat and how you live. Here is a simple checklist to to help you create an ongoing lifestyle to de-age your body.

21st Century Survival

- **Make Every Calorie Count:** Gradually decrease the quantity of foods you eat while increasing the nutrients you are taking in. Choose your meals from real foods, the best nature has to offer: raw vegetables, whole grains, fresh fruits, pulses and seeds, prepared in simple ways to preserve their innate nutritional richness.

- **Avoid Processed Foods:** Nix on junk fats, margarines, refined sugar and simple carbohydrates like most packaged breakfast cereals which tend to be depleted of essential minerals, trace elements and fibre.

- **Go Organic:** Whenever possible buy (better yet grow) organic vegetables, grains, seeds and nuts. Foods grown without chemical fertilizers help protect your body from pollution while they keep essential nutrients in good balance, on which continuing health depends.

- **Get Smart About Labels:** Read labels carefully. Don't be misled by the word 'natural' or 'no preservatives'. Watch out for references to hydrogenated fats, aluminium, colourings and preservatives and leave foods containing them on the shelves.

- **Wash Non-Organic Foods Well:** Use 1 tablespoon of baking soda to a sink full of water. Soak for 3–5 minutes to help clear acid-pollutants from vegetables and fruits.

- **Drink Clean Water:** Use a good water filter, buy purified water or the very best natural spring waters. Don't use tap water.

- **Eat Deep-Sea Fish:** The fattier the better – sardines, mackerel, wild (not farmed) salmon are full of healthy fatty acids. Stay away from cod, shellfish and most fresh-water fish. They are more likely to be chemically polluted.

- **Avoid Aluminium Cooking:** Aluminium pots and pans can leach this metal into the foods cooked in them.

- **Don't Use Irradiated Foods:** Their effects on the body are still largely unknown and highly questionable.

- **Add Superfoods To Your Diet:** Make good use of foods and herbs that are rich in natural anti-oxidants and immune-enhancers which work synergistically to protect you. These include algae, spirulina, open-celled chlorella, Australian Dunaliella Salina, bladderwrack, Irish moss, dulse, alaria, kombu and nori as well as green cereal grasses and the power mushrooms: reishi, maitake, shiitake, tremella and cordyceps.

- **Go For Greens:** Increase your intake of cruciferous vege-tables such as broccoli, cauliflower, cabbage and Brussels sprouts as well as wild green foods like nettles, dandelion and parsley. They are brimming with anti-oxidants.

- **Minimize Drugs:** Use neither prescription drugs nor over-the-counter drugs unless they are absolutely necessary, including hormone drugs. Also minimize recreational drugs such as alcohol and nicotine, and keep away from marijuana and cocaine.

- **Practise UV Protection:** Exposure to sunlight is a great ager especially now with the depletion of the ozone layer. Protect yourself.

- **Grow a Garden:** Or at the very least sprout organic seeds and grains for salads. This gives you the freshest, chemical-free foods available. And you can sprout seeds even in a tiny kitchen in a city flat.

- **Cut Down on Meat:** Not only is the breeding of live-stock on a wide scale wasteful of the earth's resources, most meat and poultry sold comes from chemically raised animals given antibiotics and much has become polluted. If you eat meat make it organic. If you eat chicken and eggs, make them free-range.

- ● **Get Enough Sleep:** Sleep is the body's great rejuvenator, it increases anti-oxidant activities to counter free radical dangers in the body, enhances the production of the anti-ageing pineal hormone melatonin and is essential to de-ageing your body.

Loving Kindness

To care for the body, to enable it to continue to de-age, it is essential that we treat life with respect and care – something which Mitsuo Koda stresses in all of his teaching. This begins with caring for oneself. Create a lifestyle where your body and your spirit get what they need to thrive – exercise, kindness, rest, stimulation, the rewards of being taken seriously and nurtured. This is something that most of us have to *learn* how to do. We are always saying 'Oh I can't take time to meditate or do autogenics,' or 'How do I make time to take long walks or pursue a hobby I love when I have so many responsibilities to fulfil?' The answer is simple and true, and it almost always takes a very long time and a lot of suffering for each of us to learn it for ourselves. Unless you take care of yourself first, making sure that you eat well and honour your inner values in the way you live, you will be incapable of caring for others properly. For me this has been – in many ways still *is* – the hardest lesson I have ever had to learn. Each of us behaves unconsciously as we have been taught to behave. If our parents happened to desert us or did not care for us very well then we somehow take on their habits about ourselves and don't look after ourselves properly either. The only way to change this is through constant awareness and continued commitment to nurturing the life within us. This in turn develops our ability to nurture others and the earth.

Life Begins Today

Today really is the first day of the rest of your life. It can be an exciting one, no matter what age you are now, what you want to change, and what dreams you want to bring into reality. Begin by making friends with the cornerstone practices of *Ten Steps to a Younger You* – contrast-hydros, autogenics, Feldenkrais, nutrient-rich/calorie-poor eating. Use them regularly to make your life work better and enhance your capacity for joy. Finally explore what you love most and begin to do it – even if you can only manage an hour or two a week to start with.

The American expert in mythology Joseph Campbell used to urge his students at Sarah Lawrence College to 'follow your bliss' and to 'participate joyously in the sorrows of the world'. It is great advice when it comes to de-ageing body and mind. By this Campbell did not mean going out of our way to have a good time or chasing rainbows. Far from it. He meant coming in touch with whatever is your particular, individual passion and then pursuing it for its own sake, simply because it brings you joy. This can be gardening, racing motor bikes, going back to university, travelling, listening to music, dancing or surfing the Net.

The whole point about following one's bliss and honouring one's passions is that doing it leads step by step down a road towards personal authenticity as well as towards the kind of fulfilment that has nothing to do with external success or the approval of society. This too is like rediscovering the joy of childhood, when for hours you could sit and perform a particular act or work with a particular skill as life unfolded moment by moment. When it comes to ongoing rejuvenation of body, mind and spirit, what can be better than that?

Food Notes

Like much of modern science, most nutrition tends to be highly reductionist. Reductionism is the world view which asserts that an effective understanding of any complex system can be gained by investigating the properties of its isolated parts. This is a serious mistake made not only by nutritionists and food scientists themselves but also by most of the food industry as well. As a result of this mistake our health suffers greatly. The science of nutrition is based on the notion that the function of a vitamin, mineral or protein is encapsulated in its chemical structure. It assumes that the body needs certain quantities of these nutrients as well as some protein, fat, carbohydrate and so forth in order to avoid gross nutritional deficiencies such as beriberi, pellagra and scurvy, and it doesn't concern itself greatly with how it gets them. It gives little thought to the importance of how they are combined in natural fresh foods.

In truth the function of a vitamin or protein or any other nutrient can only be expressed by the interaction of this nutrient with its biochemical and physiological milieu. And unless you are reasonably knowledgeable about this milieu, its function cannot be understood. The body's biochemical milieu, like fresh foods grown on healthy soils, is highly complex. It includes vitamins, minerals and other accessory factors and there is evidence that a shortage or an excess of one vitamin interferes with the utilization of another. Once you begin to split off a nutrient from the milieu in which it occurs, even if later you combine it again with all of the known factors with which it was originally linked, you greatly reduce its health-promoting potential. (This is a mistake many pill-popping longevists make when they assume they can eat anything they like as long as they take massive quantities of anti-oxidant nutrients.) An understanding of this – of the importance of fresh, *whole* foods, eaten in a state which is as close as possible to the way they are when just taken from the earth – is absolutely vital to a lifestyle which supports rejuvenation.

Take Care

It is only possible to achieve nutrient-rich/calorie-poor eating by choosing your foods very carefully and by eliminating all of the over-processed, nutritionally 'empty' foods which make up the greater part of most people's menus – from white sugar and white flour to margarines containing hydrogenated oils, soft drinks and potato crisps. Roy Walford suggests a way of eating in which people take from 10 to 25 per cent of their calories in *fats* (as opposed to the 40 per cent most people eat on a Western diet), 20 to 25 per cent of their calories in the form of *protein*, and the remainder in *complex carbohydrates* such as grains, pulses, fruits and vegetables. Such a regime needs to be rich in fresh vegetables, preferably grown organically and eaten raw to preserve as many of their nutrients as possible. It is always worth remembering that it is easier to take in a good percentage of protein by combining grains, pulses, vegetables and fruits than by eating meat.

Get Into Green

Probably the least known but most powerful foods when it comes to rejuvenation are green foods. It is time to bring them into your life. They bring you increased energy and enhance the immune system. They protect from radiation in the environment and from degenerative diseases. Go green and you can wish those annoying winter colds and 'flu goodbye. And the fun of it all is that so far advanced nutritional scientists know that green works wonders but, so far, nobody is sure just why. The chlorophyll? The enzymes? Mystery ingredients? Yes, probably, but there are many other reasons too. The very latest nutritional supplements have gone green – spirulina, chlorella, green barley, blue-green algae. Why? Because the nutrients they contain – from vitamins and minerals to trace elements, enzymes, and as yet unidentified health-promoting factors – are not only richest in green foods, they are found there in perfect balance and in a highly bio-available form. Enjoy your greens, your system simply laps them up.

Try stirring a tablespoon of dried cereal grass (for example dried wheat grass or barley grass) into a glass of juice. Or, if you have a juicer of your own, put a handful of fresh green leaves – cabbage, lettuce, nettles, comfrey – through the juicer with carrot and apple. (Go gently, the taste can be too strong for some to begin with.)

Add a teaspoon to a tablespoon of spirulina or chlorella to a glass of juice to make use of their remarkable health-enhancing properties.

Easily overlooked, watercress and parsley eaten fresh and raw are ultra-green and ultra-strong. Watercress contains more organic minerals than even spinach and has a high sulphur content which experts in natural medicine claim helps to improve the functioning of the endocrine system. Parsley is a natural diuretic and is famous for its ability to improve the functioning of the kidneys and for its anti-oxidant compounds. Both taste wonderful and make interesting bases for green salads.

The secret of using any of the green foods is to begin small and keep adding more as you get used to them. Generally speaking, the worse your diet has been before you begin the less you will like the taste of the green foods in the beginning. This is particularly true if you have always been a big sugar eater.

Meat Monitoring

Most meat contains too much fat and all meat is low in fibre. There is no necessity to eat flesh foods as part of your high-nutrient/calorie-poor diet. However, if you do choose to eat flesh foods then they should be those which have had the least processing. This excludes most meats such as beef, veal and pork, since they are very high in fat and also tend to contain a high level of chemical contaminants which you want to avoid. So opt for free-range poultry, organic meats, game and seafood, all of which are lower in saturated fats and less likely to be contaminated.

Meat and fish vary tremendously in quality depending on their freshness and on how much exposure the animals have had to chemicals, growth hormones, artificial feeds and so forth. You can choose from:

Cornish hens	game
free-range chicken	fish
organic lamb	seafood
free-range turkey	

Whatever you choose always remember that in a high-nutri-ent/calorie-poor way of eating, concentrated protein foods such as meat and fish never form the centre of a meal. Use them sparingly as side dishes: whereas once you would have had your salad in a bowl next to your steak, you will now want to have your big raw salad as the centre of the meal.

Fabulous Fruit

Not only are fruits some of the most delicious natural foods available, they also have remarkable properties for spring-cleaning the body and are excellent biochemical antidotes to the stress that ages. Because fruits contain many natural acids such as *citric* and *malic* acid, they have an acid *pH* reaction in digestion. However, since they are also a rich source of alka-line-forming minerals, their reaction in the blood is always alkaline. This reaction helps neutralize the acid by-products of stress as well as the waste products of metabolism, which are also acidic. That is why fruits are so highly prized as a means of internally cleansing the body.

Fruit contains very little protein, but it is very high in the mineral potassium which needs to be balanced with sodium for perfect health in the body. Because most people in the west eat far too much sodium in the form of table salt and an excess of protein as well (which leaches important minerals from the bones and tissues), eating fruit can help re-balance a body, improve its functioning, and make you feel more energetic as well. Finally, because fruits are naturally sweet and because we are born with an innate liking for sweet things, a dessert of fresh fruit after a meal can be tremen-dously satisfying to the palate. And there is such a variety of beautiful textures, colours and tastes to choose from – from the sensuous softness of persimmons, the super-sweetness of fresh figs, to the exhilarating crunch of the finest English apple. But remember, fruits are treats, not staples.

Venerable Vegetables

The best vegetables are those you grow yourself organically. If you are lucky enough to have a garden – even a small one

– save all your leftovers and turn them into compost for fertilizer. Even in winter you can grow some delicious salads and root vegetables in a greenhouse or under cloches. The quality of organic produce is far superior to chemically fertilized fruits and vegetables – not to mention all of the vitamins which are lost in foods when they are picked, stored, shipped and sit on shop shelves. During the summer I go to the garden to pick my vegetables, and fifteen minutes later they are gracing the dinner table. That is the best way to preserve their nutritional value as well as to experience the fullness of their flavour. If you are a flat dweller without a garden you can sprout fresh seeds and grains in jars or trays on your windowsill (see page 177).

How you treat your vegetables once you have picked them or bought them from the shops determines largely how they taste and how much of their energy-enhancing good-ness you preserve. Scrub anything that will stand up to a good scrubbing, using a brush marked *veg only*. Scrubbing vegetables is better than peeling since many of the valuable vitamins and minerals are stored directly beneath the skin. Never soak vegetables for long periods. They are better washed briefly under running water so as not to allow to leach out water-soluble vitamins. Always keep vegetables as cool as possible (even carrots and turnips are best kept in the fridge) and use them as soon as you can. When shopping for fresh vegetables, be demanding – choose your own cauli-flower and make sure it is a good one. Don't be intimidated by pushy greengrocers who want to pass you off with their leftovers before they bring their new stock out. Demand the best and you will get it. Your palate and your health will be grateful that you do.

Grand Grains

Thousands of years ago the Persian sage Zarathustra wrote in ecstatic terms about grains. 'When the light of the moon waxeth warmer,' he said, 'golden hued grains grow up from the earth during the spring.' I have always thought his words beautifully captured the richness and delight of the grain foods. When a good portion of what you eat comes from grain foods, the complex carbohydrates they contain have an effect on the brain which tends to improve your disposition, make you feel calm and brings you energy that lasts and lasts. Grains, like legumes (beans and pulses), need special handling. They should not be eaten raw. This is why many of the packaged mueslis cause digestive upset in many people. It is only by cooking them (or by sprouting or soaking them) that you break the chemical bonds, turning hard-to-digest starches into more easily digested sugars. All grains can be toasted – lightly. This process, which is called *dextrinizing*, also enhances the flavour of grains used as cereals or cooked in other recipes.

To dextrinize grains spread them on a baking sheet and pop them into an oven at 150°C (300°F) for about twenty minutes, moving them around every now and then. This is not necessary if you are going to boil them, however it does enhance the flavour and is particularly good if you want to use grains to make porridge or other hot breakfast cereals. The other important thing to remember about grains is that it is best to eat as wide a variety as possible, so if you have oat porridge at breakfast, at lunch you might choose whole rye bread or a bulgur wheat salad or brown rice. The more variety the better since each grain boasts a different balance of essential minerals and micro-nutrients.

Guide to Cooking Grains

Grain	Water (1 cup)	Cooking Time (cups)	Yield (cups)
Barley (whole)	4–5	2–3 hours	3¹/₂
Barley (flakes)	3	45–60 minutes	3
Brown rice	2–2¹/₂	1 hour	3
Buckwheat	2	20 minutes	2¹/₂
Bulgur wheat	2	15–20 minutes	2¹/₂
Couscous	1	15 minutes	2³/₄
Millet	2¹/₂–3	45–60 minutes	3¹/₂
Oats (whole groats)	5	2–3 hours	2¹/₂
Polenta	5	45–60 minutes	3¹/₂
Rye	5	2–3 hours	2
Quinoa	2	20 minutes	2¹/₂
Wild rice	3	1–1¹/₂ hours	3¹/₂
Wheat (whole-grain)	5	2–3 hours	2³/₄
Wheat flakes	2	45–60 minutes	3

Occasional Oils

It is wise not to use oils other than very small quantities (1–2 tablespoons a day) of cold-pressed soya oil and extra virgin olive oil. In heat-processed oils usable *cis* fatty acids have been chemically changed into *trans* fatty acids – junk fats – which can not only be actively harmful, but actually block the use of any *cis* fatty acids in the rest of your diet. Olive oil adds a distinctive flavour to salad dressings. It is quite heavy, though, and some people prefer a lighter oil.

The oil found in flax seed or linseed is an almost perfect balance of *linoleic* and *linolenic* acid – both the omega 6 and omega 3 fatty acids. Linoleic acid is prominent in many vegetables. Linolenic acid belongs to the omega 6 family; these are the fatty acids which are generally most prevalent in fatty fishes. What makes flax seed oil so exceptional is that it has such a high degree of the omega 3 fatty acids which are, incidentally, particularly important in fat-burning. The way to take flax seed oil is by eating the seeds themselves – flax seed oil that has been extracted is too easily made rancid. I grind flax seed in a coffee grinder and then put it into a tightly covered jar and store it in the refrigerator. It is important to go for the very best German vacuum-packed linseeds in order to make sure that the precious fatty acids which they contain are protected from rancidity (see Resources, p. 183). It is as easy as that to make sure you get all the essential fatty acids provided you steer clear of junk fats and processed oils. Your body will do the rest.

Nutritious Nuts

Fresh nuts are a good source of essential fatty acids when used in small quantities. However, the rancid oils in old nuts are harmful to the stomach. They retard pancreatic enzymes and destroy vitamins. If nuts are fresh and whole (unbroken) you can buy a kilo or so at a time and, provided they are kept airtight in a cool dry place (best in the fridge) they will keep for a few months. You can even freeze them and keep them longer than that. It is a good idea to buy a few different kinds, then if you mix them you will get a good balance of essential amino acids. You will also have more variety in your recipes. Choose from almonds, brazils, cashews, coconut (fresh or desiccated), hazels, macadamia nuts, pecans, pine kernels, pistachios, tiger nuts and walnuts.

Seductive Seeds

Be sure you buy really fresh seeds with no signs of decay. The three seeds which provide a particularly valuable combination of protein and essential fatty acids are sunflower, pumpkin and sesame. They can be ground fresh in a coffee grinder and sprinkled on salads or cereals. Other seeds worth trying, mainly for seasoning, are poppy, celery, caraway, dill, fennel and anise.

Lovely Legumes

Nutritious, economical and delicious when well-prepared, legumes – beans and pulses – are rich in complex carbo-hydrates, protein, and fibre as well as minerals and essential fatty acids. It is important to know how to handle them and to cook them well in order to avoid digestive upset. All legumes should be washed and cleared of any small pieces of stone or spoilt food. Then everything except lentils, split peas and mung beans should be soaked for at least four to six hours, preferably overnight, before cooking. The soak-water should then be thrown away and fresh water should be added. There are two ways to minimize digestive upset when cooking legumes such as beans, and I use both of them. The first is, after soaking and rinsing, put them in the freezer overnight and cook them the next day. The second is after soaking, throw the soak-water away, boil up the beans for twenty minutes, throw the boil-water away, rinse the beans, put more water plus whatever vegetables, herbs and season-ings you may be putting in with them, then cook in a covered saucepan by bringing the beans to the boil and then reducing the heat and simmering until they grow tender.

There are so many things that you can make with legumes that you could fill ten cookbooks with wonderful recipes. I like to make thick soups and casseroles of them. They are great cooked and used cold the next day as a base for a whole-meal salad. In either case I add whatever vegetables I intend to cook with the beans plus some low-salt vegetable broth powder, and whatever other seasoning I am choosing to use. I then bring the beans to the boil, and allow them to simmer for the prescribed length of time. Alternatively I will bring the beans to the boil and put them in a slow cooker or the bottom of the Aga and forget about them for six to eight hours. I sometimes cook beans overnight this way. I soak various kinds of beans, such as lima beans, black-eyed beans, kidney beans, or a mixture of them, pour the soak-water away, rinse them, then store them frozen in bags so that I can pull them out whenever I need them to make a casserole or a soup.

Many legumes sprout well, particularly lentils, mung and adzuki beans. Legumes contain a *trypsin inhibitor*, a substance which blocks the action of some of the enzymes which break down protein in your body, and because of this they must never be eaten raw. Trypsin inhibitors are destroyed when legumes are well cooked. Sprouting also neutralizes them. Here is a chart that will give you some guidelines for the cooking of legumes:

BEANS AND PULSES

Legume	Soak (1 cup)	Water (cups)	Cooking Time (hours)	Yield (cups)
Adzuki	Yes	4	3	2
Baby lima	Yes	3	2	1³/4
Black beans	Yes	5	2	2
Cassoulet	Yes	4	3¹/2	2
Chick peas	Yes	4	3¹/2	2¹/2
Kidney	Yes	3	1¹/2	2
Lentils	No	4	1	2¹/4
Lima	Yes	5	2	1¹/4
Mung	No	2¹/2	1¹/2	2
Navy	Yes	3	2¹/2	2
Pinto	Yes	3	2¹/2	2
Red	Yes	3	3¹/2	2
Split Peas	No	3	1	2¹/4

Sprout Sensation

Seeds and grains are latent powerhouses of nutritional goodness and life energy. Add water to germinate them, let them grow for a few days in your kitchen and you will harvest delicious, inexpensive fresh foods of quite phenomenal health-enhancing value. The vitamin content of seeds increases dramatically when they germinate. The vitamin C content in soya beans multiplies five times within three days of germination – a mere tablespoon of soybean sprouts contains half the recommended daily adult requirements of this vitamin. The vitamin B_2 in an oat grain rises by 1,300 per cent almost as soon as the seed sprouts and by the time tiny leaves have formed it has risen by 2,000 per cent! Some sprouted seeds and grains are believed to have anti-cancer properties, which is why they form an important part of the natural methods of treating the disease.

When you sprout a seed, enzymes which have been dormant in it spring into action, breaking down stored starch and turning it into simple natural sugars and splitting long chain proteins into amino acids. What this means is that the process of sprouting turns these seeds into foods which are very easily assimilated by your body when you eat them. Sprouts are, in effect, pre-digested. As such they have many times the nutritional efficiency of the seeds from which they have grown. They provide more nutrients, gramme for gramme, than any other natural food.

Because of the massive enzyme release which occurs when a seed or grain is sprouted the nutritional quality of a sprout is extremely good. These enzymes not only neutralize such factors as trypsin inhibitors but also destroy other substances which can be harmful such as *phytic acid*. Phytic acid, which occurs in considerable quantity in grains, particularly wheat, tends to bind minerals so that the digestive system cannot break them down for assimilation. When a grain is sprouted this mineral-binding capacity is virtually eliminated.

Another attractive thing about sprouts is their price. The basic seeds and grains are cheap and readily available in supermarkets and health food stores – chickpeas, brown lentils, mung beans, wheat grains and so forth. And since you sprout them yourself with nothing but clean water, they become an easily accessible source of organically grown fresh vegetables, even for city dwellers. In an age when most vegetables and fruits are grown on artificially fertilized soils and treated with hormones, fungicides, insecticides, preservatives and all manner of other chemicals, the home-grown-in-a-jar sprout emerges as a pristine blessing – fresh, unpolluted and ready to eat in a minute by popping them into salads or sandwiches. As such they can be a wonderful health food to any family concerned about the rising cost of food and the falling nutritional value in the average diet. Different sprouts mixed together will indeed support life all on their own. While I would never suggest that anybody live on sprouts alone I think they are an ideal addition to the table – particularly if the budget is tight.

Sea Vegetables

If you have never used the sea vegetables for cooking, this is an ideal time to begin. Not only are they delicious – imparting a wonderful, spicy flavour to soups and salads – they are the richest source of organic mineral salts in nature, particularly of iodine. Iodine is the mineral needed by the thyroid gland. As your thyroid gland is largely responsible for the body's metabolic rate, iodine is very important for energy. I like to use powdered kelp as a seasoning. It adds both flavour and minerals to salad dressings, salads, soups and so forth. I am also very fond of nori seaweed, which comes in long thin sheets or tiny flakes. It is a delicious snack food which you can eat along with a salad or at the beginning of the meal: it has a beautiful, crisp flavour. I often toast it very, very quickly by putting it under a grill for no more than 10 or 15 seconds. It is also delicious raw.

Get to know some of the other sea vegetables and start to make use of them. Your nails and hair will be strengthened by the full range of minerals and trace elements such as selenium, calcium, iodine, boron, potassium, magnesium, iron and others which are not always found in great quantities in our ordinary garden vegetables. The rest of your body will benefit too. You can use nori to wrap around everything from a sprout salad to cooked grains in order to make little pieces of vegetarian *sushi*. It's often a good idea to soak some of the other sea vegetables such as dulse, arame and hiziki for a few minutes in enough tepid water to cover them. This softens them so that they can be easily chopped to be put in to salads or added to soups. Sea vegetables are available in health-food stores and in oriental food shops. Recommended ones are:

arame	kombu
dulse	laver bread
hiziki	nori
kelp	wakami
mixed sea salad	

Special Foods
(see Resources, p. 183, for stockists)

CAROB (St John's Bread) Carob powder/flour is a superb chocolate substitute – and good for you too. Unlike chocolate, it does not contain caffeine. Instead it is full of minerals – calcium, phosphorous, iron, potassium, magnesium and silicon – as well as vitamins B_1, B_2, niacin and a little vitamin A, plus some protein. Carob powder is often sold toasted, but the best kind is raw. It is lighter in colour than the cooked kind. It can be bought from most health-food stores and used to make chocolate drinks, desserts and treats.

AGAR-AGAR This starch comes from seaweed. You can use it to make vegetarian gelatin-based sweets and salads and to thicken sauces and toppings. It comes in flakes or granules and sometimes in sheets. Soak the agar-agar in a little water to soften it before adding hot liquid to dissolve it. Use about 1 teaspoon to each cup of water or liquid.

ARROWROOT Made from the pulp of the tuberous root-stocks of a tropical American plant, arrowroot is a nutritious, easily digested food, high in calcium. When you heat it in water it thickens (use $1^1/2$ teaspoons per cup of liquid). It is better than cornstarch or cornflour for thickening gravy, fruit sauces, soups and stews.

Seasonings

MUSTARD Mustard can be bought in dry or paste form. The dry powder is sometimes useful in dressings. I think the most delicious mustards are French. They are milder and more aromatic than English mustard. Moutarde de Meaux is particularly delicious and is great in dressings for all sorts of salads. Dijon and Bordeaux are also nice.

TAHINI (preferably unroasted) A paste made from ground sesame seeds which is delicious and very nutritious. It has many uses including tahini mayonnaise, and is delicious as an addition to many seed and nut dishes.

LOW-SALT VEGETABLE BOUILLON POWDER
This is something I use a lot to season just about everything.
Use it for soup stocks, to flavour pizzas, grains like brown
rice and kasha, and even salad dressings, stews and
casseroles. It is my favourite of all seasonings. The very best
is Marigold's Low-Salt Swiss Vegetable Bouillon. I even take
it with me when I travel.

YEAST EXTRACT This can be used as a substitute for
'vegetable bouillon'. It is rich in B Complex vitamins, but
very salty, so it should also be used in moderation.

FOOD YEAST This is sometimes called primary yeast or
nutritional yeast. It is *not* brewers' yeast which is a by-prod-
uct of beer making. Food yeast is grown specifically to be
used as a flavouring. It is light yellow-beige and slightly spiky
in its texture, and is good to add to soups, sauces, cheeses
and dips. You can even sprinkle it on popcorn.

Hormone Helpers

Many fresh foods are rich in plant hormones. The fresher
they are the better: yams, peas, papayas, bananas, cucumbers,
raw nuts, bee pollen, sprouted seeds and grains and the
herbs licorice root, alfalfa, red clover, sage, sarsaparilla and
sassafras. Raw fruits and vegetables, the green vegetable
juices, in particular, figs and garlic, dates, avocados, grapes,
apples, chlorella, seaweed and wheat germ can all be helpful
in countering menopausal and menstrual problems. Grapes,
cherries, citrus fruits and red clover are excellent sources of
the *bioflavonoids* which also have weak oestrogenic activity
and have shown themselves to be useful in countering hot
flushes and mood swings and in helping to prevent heavy or
irregular menstrual flow. Plant foods high in phyto-sterols are

good insurance against cancer, and the anti-oxidants in fresh plant foods offer protection against cancer too. These include vitamin C from fresh fruits and vegetables, vitamin E in fresh whole grains, and vitamin A from fish liver and from the beta carotene in carrots, tomatoes, apricots and red and yellow peppers. The fibre found in plants is protective against cancer via another mechanism. Breast cancer is closely related to oestrogen levels as well as to the consumption of high levels of meat and fat. Women on a vegetarian diet high in fibre excrete a much higher level of oestrogen than other women and have much lower blood levels of these hormones. In Britain and the United States the use of milk products too has been correlated with breast cancer. Sea plants and green vegetables, spirulina and chlorella are far better sources of calcium than cheese and milk. Some of the best products of all are the soya-based foods from the Orient, together with naturally fermented foods – often of Japanese origin.

TOFU Its other name is bean curd. This white, bland soft food made from soya beans is easy to digest, high in protein, low in calories and fat, cheap, and you can use it for just about anything. It behaves a bit like a sponge which will absorb whatever flavour you soak it in. When you cook it, it becomes firmer. You can mix it with herbs, make sauces or low-fat mayonnaise from it, dips for vegetables, pizza toppings and stir-fries. You can even substitute it for cheese in some of your favourite recipes – except that it doesn't melt under the grill. Buy it in the supermarket, health food store or Oriental food shop and keep it sitting in water in the fridge so it doesn't dry out.

MISO A fermented soybean paste which is rich in digestive enzymes and high in protein. Miso comes in many flavours and ranges in colour from the sweet pale tan varieties to the dark rich brown and red misos. Some misos are made from barley, others from rice or chickpeas. In texture they resemble a soft nut butter which can be spread on bread or added to soups, grain dishes and casseroles, and it makes a delicious addition to dips for crudités and salad dressings. Miso makes a wonderful instant broth – simply put a heaped teaspoon to tablespoon of miso in the bottom of a large cup or bowl and pour boiling water over it. You can then add sea vegetables such as flaked nori or spirulina or other green foods to taste.

TAMARI This is a type of soya sauce made from fermented soya beans, but unlike ordinary soya sauce it contains no wheat, although it does contain sea salt so it should be used in moderation. It is good for giving a 'Chinese' taste to dishes as well as a rich flavour to bland dressings or sauces.

SOYA FLOUR Made from cooked, ground soybeans, soya flour is sometimes added to grain-based flours to increase their protein content. It can be used to make soya milk and soya cheese.

SOYA MILK Made from cooked, ground and strained soybeans this is often used for bottle-fed infants who are allergic to cow's milk. I use it as a substitute for milk on cereals and in recipes. You can make your own very cheaply. I prefer to do this since ready-made varieties are often packed in aluminium-lined cartons and it is best to avoid aluminium.

Herbal Helpmates

The magicians of life-generating cooking, fresh herbs can transform a humble recipe into a pasha's delight. I use them constantly, lavishly, and occasionally with utter abandon. I have been known to add as many as seven different leafy herbs to a simple green salad which becomes more of a herb salad than a green salad by the time I have finished. I grow most of my herbs in the garden because there is something about freshness which you can't recapture from the dried varieties. With fresh herbs you needn't worry much about choosing the wrong ones. Some of my favourites for salads include lovage (which I also use to season many salad dressings), basil, dill, the mints, winter savory, fennel, chives and the parsleys. In the summer I cull them from the garden. Some I dry by hanging from beams in the kitchen for a few days and then store them in airtight jars for winter use. Others – the more succulent herbs such as parsley, basil and chives – can be deep frozen in sprigs then simply chopped and used when needed. If you live in a flat or don't have a garden you can grow herbs in pots in the kitchen window where they lend their beauty to the room as well as offering a constant supply of culinary delights. Thyme, marjoram and winter savory will grow beautifully in pots indoors over the winter. So will parsley. Once you begin to play about with herb magic you will probably find, as I have, that you never want to be without these lovely plants. Here are some of the most common herbs and what I find them useful for:

BASIL I probably use this herb far too much because it is available only in the summer months and because it is simply so lovely. It has a distinctive flavour which is an ideal garnish for tomatoes or, in larger amounts, mixed into a green salad. Use the leaves whole for the best possible flavour.

CHERVIL This herb is a cousin to parsley, with a delicate aniseed flavour. We use it lavishly in salads. It mixes particularly well with chives, tarragon and parsley.

CHIVES More beautiful in looks than in flavour, I think, chives are great for sprinkling onto sunflower wafers or in seed cheeses. I do not find them strong enough for most salads and prefer spring onions instead, or a little chopped shallot.

DILL Dill goes wonderfully with dressings, cucumbers, and beetroot and apple salads, and has a gentle, delicate flavour which reminds me of quiet afternoons under sun-shaded willows.

FENNEL This lacy, aniseed-flavoured herb grows to immense height in the summer months. It goes well with salsify salads and with cucumbers, tomatoes and in vegetable loaves. It is also a lovely decorative herb to place around the edge of a dish of salads.

LOVAGE Perhaps the most under-rated of the common herbs, lovage is wonderful mixed with the mints and yoghurt as the base of a herbal salad dressing which is as beautiful in colour as it is in flavour. I also use lots of it in my dish salads.

MARJORAM This herb comes in many variations – sweet marjoram, pot marjoram, winter marjoram, golden marjoram. Each is a little different. The sweet variety is lovely with plain green salads and goes well with tomatoes and Mediterranean vegetables. Oregano is a wild marjoram akin to our winter variety.

THE MINTS There are even more varieties than the marjorams – spearmint, peppermint, apple mint, pineapple mint, ginger mint, eau de cologne mint. I use spearmint and apple mint in green salads and many dressings. Pineapple mint with its splendid variegated leaves makes a wonderful garnish for fruit salads, drinks and also salad platters. Ginger mint is great in summer drinks, sorbets and punches.

PARSLEY This common herb comes in two main varieties – fine and broad leaf. For most raw dishes we prefer the broadleaf parsley because it is more delicate and pleasant to munch. Both have a rich 'green' flavour which works well with other herbs. It is great chopped in patties and loaves, in green salads and for dressings as well as being a lovely garnish for almost any dish.

SAGE This herb has a strong individual flavour and a particular affinity for onions. It is good in savoury nut dishes and adds flavour to seed and nut ferments.

THYME Thyme comes in many varieties, some of which are much richer in flavour than others, but all have a wonderful, warming, sweet flavour which enhances peppers, courgettes and nut dishes as well as giving a unique flavour to sprout salads.

Eating Out

Eating out and sticking to nutrient-rich/calorie-poor eating is not as great a challenge as you might imagine. If the worst comes to the worst you can even plunder a salad bar in a fast-food restaurant if you choose the bits and pieces carefully. The better restaurants make life a great deal easier. These days restaurant managers are not at all taken aback by someone making special dietary requests. When it is feasible call ahead and speak to the chef or manager, explaining that you do not eat white flour, sugar or free-fats and asking what in particular they would suggest from their menu. Steer clear of foods that are fried, creamed, au gratin or sautéed. Ask if they will prepare something for you without oil, and always request that any sauces come as side-dishes – not poured over the food that you have ordered. Almost every decent restaurant these days has fresh fruit for dessert. Many restaurants have vegetarian main dishes but get them to leave off the greasy cheese or sour cream. If you find one that doesn't have vegetarian dishes, and you don't want to eat fish or meat, order a soup or a salad as a first course and a plate of steamed or wok-fried vegetables, or two or three starters to follow. If you fancy a chef's salad, simply ask them to leave the meat and cheese off it and request that they use lemon juice or vinegar, garlic and pepper instead of oil as salad dressing. You can also order a plate of vegetables and ask that the chef does not use any oil or butter in their preparation.

When you are invited out to dinner at someone's house, explain to your hosts that you do not eat white flour, sugar or processed oils, and if necessary, have something to eat before you go so you are not too hungry.

Slow and Steady

The most important thing to remember is that the lifestyle changes you are instigating do not belong to some rigid programme where you have to grit your teeth and bear it. Far from it. They are the means by which, given time, you can rediscover your own strength, vitality and pathway to freedom. This pathway will only be found slowly and steadily over time as you discover what works best for you and make readjustments to suit you. There will be moments when the general principles of Ten Steps to a Younger You will be forgotten. These times are of no great significance. If one morning you sit down and eat half a pound of chocolate, it is no big deal. Indeed, by being aware of how it makes you feel both then and afterwards, such an experience can empower you even further. For you are in control and it is you who makes the choices about your own life and health. The freedom that comes with discovering this is of an order which cannot be described. It is something you must discover for yourself.

Recipes

Here are some of my favourite recipes for the Clean Sweep Diet (and indeed for afterwards). Many serve one person. Others serve as many as four. They can be cut down if you are cooking for only yourself or served to a family as part of their ordinary meals. The soups and stews freeze well and can be put into individual containers and frozen for quick use later.

C = *cupful*
tbs = *tablespoonful*
tsp = *teaspoonful*

Energy Shakes

Put any fresh fruit of your choice in a blender, add 175 ml (6 fluid ounces) or more of spring water plus your choice of green leaves or superfoods, and blend. Serve immediately. Good combinations: apple and banana, mixed berries, orange and pineapple, watermelon.

Fruit and Vegetable Juices

Put the fruits and vegetables of your choice plus green leaves through a centrifugal juice extractor and serve immediately. Alternatively you can leave out the green leaves and instead add 1/2 teaspoon (or more) of a green superfood such as powdered green barley, spirulina, chlorella, or Pure Synergy (see Resources, p. 185), and stir well. Good combinations include: carrot and apple; beetroot, carrot and apple; celery and tomato.

Barley Pilaff

A delicious baked dish. It is made from pot barley, not from pearl barley. Barley is also excellent in soups.

2 onions, finely chopped
1 tsp olive oil
1 C pot barley
1^1/$_2$ C spring water
1 tbs vegetable bouillon powder
1 tbs dill, chopped
2 cloves of garlic, finely chopped

Sauté the onions in the oil until translucent, then add the barley to the pan and stir well. Remove from the heat and add the remaining ingredients (including the water, boiled in a kettle). Place in a lightly oiled oven dish and bake in a moderate oven for half an hour. Check to see if you need to add a little more water. Serve immediately.

Brown Rice

Rice cooked in this manner is so delicious that it is a worth-while dish in itself. It needs no special sauces or condiments to make it work.

1 C brown rice
2–3 C spring water
2 tsp vegetable bouillon powder
3 tbs fresh parsley, chopped
1 tsp marjoram, chopped
2 cloves garlic, finely chopped (optional)

Wash the rice three times under running water and put into a saucepan. Boil the water in a kettle and pour over the rice. Add seasonings, except for the parsley. Bring to the boil and cook gently for 45 minutes or until all the liquid has been absorbed. Garnish with parsley and serve. If you double the quantities used here you can keep some back and make a delicious rice salad the next day.

Garden Crunch Salad

I like to use purple sprouting broccoli from the garden in this, but the ordinary green variety or a mixture of both is just as good.

1/2 iceberg lettuce
2 or 3 broccoli stalks (use the stems as well as the tops)
1 C finely shredded red cabbage
2–3 tomatoes
several mushrooms
handful of fresh garden peas
1 shallot or small red onion
a handful of toasted pumpkin seeds

Shred the lettuce and place in a bowl. Add the broccoli, their tops broken into small pieces and the stems peeled and sliced crosswise. Shred the red cabbage really finely, chop the tomatoes and slice the mushrooms. Add the peas and the shallot or onion cut into rings. Toss all the ingredients together and top with toasted pumpkin seeds.

Kasha

Kasha has been a favourite for me ever since a Russian lover taught me how to make this traditional dish.

2 C buckwheat groats
spring water to cover
2 teaspoons vegetable bouillon powder
2 tbs fresh parsley or other herbs, chopped
1 clove garlic, crushed

Place the buckwheat in a heavy-bottomed pan and roast it dry over a medium heat while stirring with a wooden spoon. As it begins to darken, pour hot water over it and add the vegetable bouillon powder, garlic and 1 teaspoon of the herbs. Cover and simmer very slowly for about 15–20 minutes until all the liquid has been absorbed. Serve sprinkled with the remaining herbs or pour a light gravy over the top.

Polenta

Polenta is a dish made from cornmeal. I particularly like it served with a salad dressed with a spicy sauce.

3 C spring water
1 C cornmeal
2 tsp vegetable bouillon powder

Heat the water in a kettle. Pour boiling water over the cornmeal and blend into a paste with the vegetable bouillon powder. Stir until smooth and cook very gently until all the liquid has been absorbed. Cool and drop by the spoonful on to a very lightly oiled baking sheet and grill until brown, turning once.

Russian Red Stir Fry

A very light refreshing cabbage dish which is quick and easy to prepare.

3/4 red cabbage or Savoy cabbage
225g (1/2 lb) white turnip
1 tbs olive oil
4 spring onions, chopped finely
1 tbs soy sauce
1 tbs tomato purée
1 tsp cumin seeds
1 tsp paprika
1 tsp vegetable bouillon powder
freshly ground black pepper

Wash the cabbage and shred finely. Grate the turnip finely. Heat the oil in a large saucepan or wok, and fry the cabbage-turnip mixture together with the spring onions over a high heat for three minutes. Add the remaining ingredients (including a little spring or filtered water if necessary) and cook for a further five minutes. Season with black pepper and serve immediately.

Sprout Salad

This simple living salad can be completely transformed depending on the kind of dressing you serve it with. Experiment with a tofu mayonnaise or a light herb dressing.

1 C lentil sprouts
1 C fenugreek sprouts
1 C alfalfa sprouts
1 C Chinese leaves, shredded finely
3 carrots, sliced in paper-thin rounds
4 tomatoes, diced

Mix the ingredients together and toss with your favourite dressing. Serve immediately.

Tofu Dip

1 C tofu
juice of 1 lemon
1 tsp wholegrain Meaux mustard
vegetable bouillon powder to taste
fresh basil
mint

Thoroughly combine all the ingredients in the food processor.

Tofu Mayonnaise

2 C tofu
2 cloves of garlic
juice of 3 lemons
1 tbs vegetable bouillon powder
2 tsp curry powder
2 tsp onion powder
pinch of salt

Put all the ingredients in a food processor and blend until smooth. If it is too thick, add a little water.

Tofu Vinaigrette

This is particularly nice served with artichokes.

3/4 C tofu
3 tbs wine vinegar
juice of 2 lemons
1 tbs Dijon mustard
1 clove garlic, crushed
salt and pepper, finely ground

Place all ingredients in a blender and process.

Wild Carrot Dressing

This dressing is one of my favourites. It goes well either on a salad or on steamed vegetables.

3 large carrots, washed and cut into small pieces
10 chives, chopped finely
1 tsp vegetable bouillon powder
1 C blanched almonds (preferably soaked overnight in
    1–2 C spring or filtered water)
2 tsp chopped parsley

Put all the ingredients into a food processor or blender and blend with as much water as you need to make the dressing the consistency you want. It's best to leave it thick if you want to use it as a dip, or make it thinner as a dressing to pour over salads.

Winter Chunk Salad

Slaws are ideal winter salads because in the cold months, when lettuce is hard to come by, cabbage is a staple. Another perfect ingredient for the winter season is sprouted seeds and beans. For this salad you simply combine whatever winter vegetables and sprouts you have available and toss them together with a creamy tofu dressing.

Select three of the following and grate: carrots, turnip, Jerusalem artichoke, kohlrabi, white radish, beetroot.
Add a handful of mixed sprouts: mung, lentil, wheat, alfalfa, fenugreek or chick peas. Combine with a handful of raisins.

SPROUTING

All you need to start your own indoor germinating 'factory' are a few old jars, some pure water, fresh seeds/grains/pulses, and an area of your kitchen or a windowsill which is not absolutely freezing.

Home-made sprouters There are two main ways to sprout seeds – in jars and in seed trays. Let's look at the traditional way first, then at the way we find easiest and best.

A simple and cheap sprouter can be anything from a bucket to a polythene bag. The traditional sprouter is a wide-mouthed glass jar. Some people like to make it all neat by covering the jar with a cheesecloth or a nylon or wire mesh and securing it with a rubber band, or using a mason jar with a screw-on rim to keep the cheesecloth in place. But I find the easiest and least fussy way is simply to use open jars and to cover a row of them with a tea towel to prevent dust and insects from getting in.

Start Here

- Put the seed/grain/pulse of your choice, for example mung, in a large sieve. (For the amount to use see the chart on page 181, and remember that most sprouts give a volume about eight times that of the dry seeds/grains/pulses.) Remove any small stones, broken seeds or loose husks and rinse your sprouts well.
- Put the seeds in a jar and cover with a few inches of pure water. Rinsing can be done in tap water, but the initial soak, where the seeds absorb a lot of water to set their enzymes in action, is best done in spring, filtered or boiled and then cooled water, as the chlorine in tap water can inhibit germination – and is also not very good for you.
- Leave your sprouts to soak overnight, or as long as is needed.
- Pour off the soak-water – if none remains then you still have thirsty beans on your hands, so give them more water to absorb. The soak-water is good for watering houseplants. Some people like to use it in soups or drink it straight, but I find it extremely bitter. Also, the soak-water from some beans and grains contains *phytates* – nature's insecticides, which protect the vulnerable seeds in the soil from invasion by micro-organisms. These phytates interfere with certain biological functions in the body, including the absorption of many minerals (notably zinc, magnesium and calcium), and are therefore best avoided. The soak-water from wheat, however, known as 'rejuvelac', makes a wonderful liquid for preparing fermented cheese and is very good for you.

- Rinse the seeds, either by pouring water through the cheesecloth top, swilling it around and pouring it off – several times – or by tipping the seeds out of the open-topped jars into a large sieve and rinsing them well under the tap before replacing them in the jar. Be sure that they are well drained either way, as too much water may cause them to rot. The cheesecloth-covered jars can be left tilted in a dish drainer to allow all the water to run out. Repeat this morning and night for most sprouts. During a very hot spell they may need a midday rinse too.

- Return the sprouter to a reasonably warm place. This can be under the sink, in an airing cupboard or just in a corner not too far from a radiator. Sprouts grow fastest and best without light and in a temperature of about 21°C (70°F).

- After about 3–5 days your sprouts will be ready for a dose of chlorophyll if you want to give them one. Alfalfa thrive on a little sunlight after they've grown for two or three days, but mung beans, fenugreek and lentils are best off without it. Place them in the sunshine – a sunny windowsill is ideal – and watch them develop little green leaves. Be sure that they are kept moist and that they don't get too hot and roast!

- After a few hours in the sun most sprouts are ready to be eaten. Optimum vitamin content occurs 50–96 hours after germination begins. They should be rinsed and eaten straight away or stored in the refrigerator in an airtight container or sealed polythene bag. Some people dislike the taste of seed hulls such as those that come with mung sprouts. To remove them simply place the sprouts in a bowl and cover with water. Stir the sprouts gently. The seed hulls will float to the top and can be skimmed off with your hand.

Make it big

Now for my favourite and simplified method, using seed trays. I find that, with the great demands made by my family for living foods, the jar method simply doesn't produce enough. Also, for sprouted seeds, you have to rinse twice a day, while tray sprouts need only a splash of water once each day. This is a very simple and easy way to grow very large quantities.

Take a few small seed trays (the kind gardeners use to grow seedlings, with fine holes in the bottom for drainage). When germinating very tiny seeds such as alfalfa you will need to line your seed tray with damp, plain white kitchen paper. For larger seeds, the trays do not need to be lined. Place the trays in a larger tray to catch the water that drains from them. Soak the seeds/grains/pulses overnight as in the jar method, then rinse them well and spread them a few layers deep in each of the trays. Spray the seeds with water (preferably by using a spray bottle) and leave in a warm place. Check the seeds each day and spray them again if they seem dry. If the seeds get too wet they will rot, so be careful not to overwater them. Larger seeds such as chickpeas, lentils and mung beans need to be gently turned over with your hand once a day to ensure that the seeds underneath are not suffocated. Alfalfa seeds can be simply sprinkled on damp paper towels and left alone. After four or five days they will have grown into a thick green carpet. Don't forget to put the sprouts in some sunlight for a day or so to develop lots of chlorophyll. When the seeds are ready, harvest them, rinse them well in a sieve and put them in an airtight container or sealed polythene bag until you want them. To make the next batch, rinse the trays well and begin again.

Tips and tricks

Some sprouts are more difficult to grow than others, but usually if seeds fail to germinate at all it is because they are too old and no longer viable. It is always worth buying top-quality seeds because, after removing dead and broken seeds, and taking germinating failures into account, they work out better value than cheaper ones. Also try to avoid seeds treated with insecticide/fungicide mixtures such as those which are sold in gardening shops and some nurseries. Health-food shops and wholefood emporiums are usually your best bet. At wholefood stores you can buy seeds very cheaply for sprouting in bulk. It is fun to experiment with growing all kinds of sprouts, from radish seeds to soya beans, but do avoid plants whose greens are known to be poisonous such as the deadly nightshade family, potato and tomato seeds. Also avoid kidney beans, as they are poisonous raw.

Some of the easiest seeds to begin with are alfalfa, adzuki (aduki) beans, mung beans, lentils, fenugreek, radish, chickpeas and wheat. Others include sunflower, pumpkin or sesame seeds, buckwheat, flax, mint, red clover and triticale. These last can sometimes be difficult to find or to sprout – the 'seeds' must be in their hulls and the nuts must be really fresh and undamaged. Good luck!

Variety	Soak Time	Dry Measure	Days to Harvest	Sprouting Tips
Alfalfa	Overnight	3tbs	4–5	Grow on wet paper towel – place in light for last 24 hrs
Chickpea	Up to 24 hours	2C	3–4	Needs long soak, renew water twice during soak
Fenugreek	Overnight	$1/2$C	3–5	Pungent flavour
Lentil	Overnight	1C	3–5	Earthy flavour
Mung	Overnight	$3/4$C	3–5	Grow in the dark – place in light for last 24 hours

Sprouting Cereal Grasses

You will need:

a seed-tray, or a kitchen tray will do
good organic potting compost
8–10 layers of newspaper
sheet of plastic to cover the tray
seed – hard red winter wheat or buckwheat, barley etc.

How to sprout:

1. Soak approximately 1 cup of seed for 12 hours in enough water to cover it well. Pour off the water and allow to drain for a further 12 hours.

2. Half-fill the seed-tray with compost (so that the compost comes halfway up the sides of the tray), level the surface and spray with a fine spray. Make sure you do not soak the compost.

3. Place the soaked seeds on the wet soil so that the seeds are evenly spread and not on top of each other.

4. Soak the newspaper thoroughly, cut it to the size of the seed tray and cover the seeds. Place the plastic on top of the newspaper.

5. Leave the tray in a well ventilated, not over-warm room for 3 days.

6. At the end of 3 days remove the plastic and newspaper and put the trays somewhere where they will get plenty of light – a sunny windowsill for instance – and water them once a day, making sure you do not soak the soil.

7. In about 5–8 days the plants should be 15–20 cm (6–8 in) high and standing tall and green. They are then ready to cut.

8. Cut the greens close to the soil with a sharp knife. They can be kept in the fridge in plastic bags for several days.

Cereal grasses can be grown all the year round wherever you live and regardless of whether or not you have a garden. Use organic seed, which should be available from good health-food stores.

Resources

Autogenic Training: To work with a trained practitioner, or to find a trained practitioner local to you, contact the British Autogenic Society, Royal London Homoeopathic Hospital, Great Ormond Street, London, WC1N 3HR. Tel: 0171 713 6336. Website: www.autogenic-therapy.org.uk

Bonsoy Soya Milk: A particularly good soya milk, unusual in that it is not packed in aluminium. It can be purchased from Freshlands, 196 Old Street, London, EC1V 9FR. Tel: 0207 250 1708. Or from Wild Oats, 210 Westbourne Grove, London, W11 2RH. Tel: 0207 229 1063.

Chlorella: See Green Supplements.

Digestive Enzymes: Good digestive enzymes from plant sources are available from BioCare. Polyzyme Forte is a very strong, broad-spectrum digestive enzyme, Digestaid is excellent for more general consumption, and Biocidin Forte, taken by those with low blood-sugar problems, is traditionally used to help maintain the balance of intestinal flora. Carbozyme aids the digestion of beans and pulses to prevent flatulence. They are available from BioCare Ltd, Lakeside, 180 Lifford Lane, Kings Norton, Birmingham B30 3NU. Tel: 0121 433 3727. Fax: 0121 433 3879. e-mail: biocare@biocare.co.uk

Feldenkrais: To find a practitioner local to you in the UK contact: The Feldenkrais Guild, PO Box 370, London, N10 3XA. Tel: 07000 785506. Email: enquires@feldenkrais.co.uk Website: www.feldenkrais.co.uk

Green Supplements: Lifestream Spirulina, Pure Synergy and other good green products are available mail order from Xynergy Health Products, Elsted, Midhurst, West Sussex GU29 0JT. Tel: 01730 813642. Fax: 01730 815109 Website: www.xynergy.co.uk Pure Synergy is simply the best nutritional supplement I have ever seen, a mix of sixty-two organically grown superfoods working together synergistically to support life-energy in its purest form.

Chlorella is available in vegi-capsule form from Solgar Vitamin & Herb, who also do an excellent green supplement "Earth Source Green & More" in powder or tablet form. For your local stockist contact:

Solgar Vitamin & Herb, Aldbury, Tring, Herts, HP23 5PT. Tel: 01442 890355. Fax: 01442 890366. Website: www.solgar.com

Herb Teas: Some of my favourite blends include Cinnamon Rose, Orange Zinger, and Emperor's Choice by Celestial Seasonings: Warm & Spicy by Symmingtons; and Creamy Carob French Vanilla. Yogi Tea, by Golden Temple Products, is a strong spicy blend, perfect as a coffee replacement. Green tea is available from health food stores and Oriental supermarkets.

Koda Clinic: Dr Mitsuo Koda can be contacted at: Dr Koda's Clinic, 2–228 Sakuragaoka, Yao-shi, Osaka 581, Japan. Tel: 00 81 729 22 5300.

Linseed Oil (Flaxseed Oil): In capsule form is available mail order from BioCare Ltd, Lakeside, 180 Lifford Lane, Kings Norton, Birmingham, West Midlands, B30 3NU. Tel: 0121 433 3727. Fax: 0121 433 3879. e-mail: biocare@biocare.co.uk. Vacuum-packed whole linseeds (flaxseeds) are available in most health-food stores. I use Linusit Gold as they are well packed and fresh.

Living Foods Residential Courses: Naturopath Elaine Bruce has spent eighteen years working with living foods as a tool for healing and teaching how to make delicious recipes. Complete course one week: A–Z of healing, gentle approach to detoxification, weight normalisation, long-lasting disease resistance and high energy levels etc. Also taster weekends: everything you need to know to set up your own Living Foods Kitchen. Small groups, individual attention, high quality organic produce. Contact Elaine Bruce, Holmleigh, Gravel Hill, Ludlow SY8 1QS. Tel: 01584 875308. Website: www.living-foods.co.uk

Marigold Swiss Vegetable Bouillon Powder: This instant broth made from vegetables and sea salt comes in regular, low-salt, vegan and organic varieties. It is available from health food stores, or direct from Marigold Foods, 102 Camley Street, London, NW1 0PF. Tel: 0207 388 4515. Fax: 0207 388 4516.

Natural Tranquillizers: Valerian and Passiflora are widely available from health food stores or by mail order from: Bioforce (UK) Ltd, 2 Brewster Place, Irvine, Ayrshire KA11 5DD. Tel: 01294 277344. Fax: 01294 277922. Website: www.bioforce.co.uk

An excellent supplier of tinctures, fluid extracts, loose dried herbs and the Schoenenberger plant juices is: Phyto Products Ltd, Park Works, Park Road, Mansfield Woodhouse, Nottinghamshire, NG19 8EF. Tel: 01623 644334. Fax: 01623 657232. e-mail: info@phyto.co.uk (Minimum order £20.)

Solgar Vitamins & Herb also do a good selection of herbs, available from most health-food stores and some chemists. For your nearest stockist contact: Solgar Vitamin & Herb, Aldbury, Tring, Herts HP23 5PT. Tel: 01442 890355. Fax: 01442 890366. Website: www.solgar.com

Organic Foods: The Soil Association publishes a regularly updated national directory of farm shops and box schemes called Where to Buy Organic Foods that costs £5 including postage from: The Soil Association, Bristol House, 40–56 Victoria Street, Bristol BS1 6BY. Tel: 0117 929 0661. Fax: 0117 925 2504. e-mail: info@soilassociation.org Website: www.soilassociation.org

Organics Direct: Offers a nationwide home delivery service of fresh vegetables and fruits, delicious breads, juices, sprouts, fresh soups, ready-made meals, snacks and baby foods. They also sell the state-of-the-art 2001 Champion Juicer and the 2002 Health Smart Juice Extractor for beginners. They even sell organic wines – all shipped to you within 24 hours. Organics Direct, 1–7 Willow Street, London EC2A 4BH. Tel: 0207 729 2828. Fax: 0207 613 5800. Website: www.organicsdirect.com. You can order online.

Clearspring: Supply organic foods and natural remedies as well as macrobiotic foods – mail order. They have a good range of herbal teas, organic grains, whole seeds for spouting, dried fruits, pulses, nut butters, Soya and vegetable products, sea vegetables, drinks and Bioforce herb tinctures. Write to them for a catalogue: Clearspring, Unit 19a, Acton Park Estate, London W3 7QE. Telephone 0208 746 0152. Fax 0208 811 8893. You can order by telephone, fax, post or shop online at www.clearspring.co.uk.

Organic Meat: Good quality organic beef, pork, bacon, lamb, chicken, turkey, duck and geese, a variety of types of sausage, all dairy products, vegetables and organic groceries (2000 lines), are available mail order from: Longwood Farm Organic Meats, Tudenham St Mary, Bury St Edmunds, Suffolk IP28 6TB. Tel: 01638 717120. Fax: 01638 717120.

Pure Synergy: See Green Supplements.

Sea plants for cooking and salads: Such as kelp, dulse, nori, kombu and wakami can be bought from Japanese grocers or macrobiotic health shops.

Ultra Clear Plus: This is a metabolic clearing programme, which contains nutrients to specifically support the body's biochemical detoxification process. It is only available through your nutritionist or healthcare practitioner. Contact: The Nutri Centre, 7 Park Crescent, London W1N 3HE. Tel: 0207 436 5122. Fax: 0207 436 5122. e-mail: enq@nutricentre.com Website: www.nutricentre.co.uk

Water: Friends of the Earth have an excellent free booklet called Water Pollution. Contact: Friends of the Earth, 26–28 Underwood Street, London N1 7JQ. Tel: 0207 490 1555. Fax: 0207 490 0881.

Wheatgrass juice: In powdered form is available from The Nutri Centre on the lower ground floor of the Hale Clinic. The Nutri Centre has the finest selection of nutritional products under one roof in Britain. It is also able to supply homeopathic products, herbal, Ayurvedic and biochemical products, flower remedies, essential oils, skincare and dental products and have an extensive selection of books including Leslie Kentonís. They also have an excellent selection of green supplements, all available through a good mail order service. For details contact: The Nutri Centre, 7 Park Crescent, London W1N 3HE. Tel: 0207 436 5122. Fax: 0207 436 5171. e-mail: enq@nutricentre.com Website: www.nutricentre.co.uk

More from Leslie Kenton

Leslie lectures and teaches workshops throughout the world on health, authentic power, energy, creativity, shamanism and spirituality. There are two companies who organize workshops for her in Britain: Bright Ideas provides workshops on health, energy and personal empowerment. They also book Leslie for lectures and individually tailored seminars when these are requested. For further information contact Bright Ideas: Tel (in the UK) 08700 783783, or email LK@bright-idea.co.uk. The Sacred Trust organizes Leslie's residential and non-residential workshops on freedom, spirituality, creativity and shamanism. For further information contact The Sacret Trust, PO Box 603, Bath BA1 2ZU. Tel: 01225 852615. Fax: 01225 858961.

Leslie's audio tapes including *10 Steps to a New You*, as well as her videos including *10 Day Clean Up Plan*, *Ageless Ageing*, *Lean Revolution*, *10 Day De-Stress Plan* and *Cellulite Revolution* can be ordered from QED Recording Services Ltd, Lancaster Road, New Barnet, Hertfordshire EN4 8AS. Tel: 0181 441 7722. Fax: 0181 441 0777; email: lesliekenton@qed-productions.com

If you want to know about Leslie's personal appearances, forthcoming books, videos, workshops and projects, please visit her website for worldwide information:
http://www.qed-productions/lesliekenton.htm

You can also write to her care of QED at the above address enclosing a stamped, self-addressed A4-sized envelope.

Further Reading

DE-AGEING

Maximum Life Span, Roy Walford, Norton, New York, 1983

The Retardation of Aging And Disease by Dietary Restriction, Roy Walford and Richard Weindruch, Springfield, Illinois, 1988.

The Anti-Ageing Plan, Roy Walford and Lisa Walford, Four Walls Eight Windows, New York/London, 1994

Prolongevity II, Albert Rosenfeld, Alfred A Knopf, Acorn Books, New York, 1977

Secrets of Life Extension, John Mann, Bantam, Harbor Publishing, San Francisco, 1980

Your Personal Life Extension Program, Saul Kent, Morrow, 1985

Experimental and Clinical Intervention in Ageing, Richard F Walker and Ralph L Cooper, Marcel Dekker, 1983

Intervention in the Aging Process, Parts A and B, William Regelson and F Marot Sinex (eds), Alan R Liss, 1983

Longevity 2 – Past, Present, Future, Johan Bjorksten, Bjorksten Research Foundation, 1986

Biological Aging Measurement, Ward Dean MD, The Centre for Bio-Gerontology, Los Angeles, 1988

The New Ageless Ageing, Leslie Kenton, Vermilion, London, 1995

Reversing Heart Disease, Dean Ornish MD, Century, New York, 1990

Free Radicals in Aging, Byung P. Yu, CRC Press, Bocaraton, Florida, 1993

Modulations of Aging Process by Dietary Restriction, edited by Byung P. Yu, CRC Press, Bocaraton, Florida, 1994

FOOD, HEALTH & WEIGHT LOSS

Fasting and Eating for Health, A Medical Doctor's Guide To Conquering Disease, Joel Fuhrman MD, St Martin's Press, New York, 1995

The British Medical Association Guide to Medicines and Drugs, Colour Library Books, Dorling Kindersley, London, 1992

Mind Food & Smart Pills, Ross Pelton with Taffy Clarke Pelton, Doubleday, New York, 1989

The Nutrition Desk Reference, by Robert H Garrison and Elizabeth Somer, Keats Publishing, New Canaan, Connecticut, 1985

Staying Healthy With Nutrition, by Eason M Haas MD, Celestial Arts, California, 1992

Healing With Whole Foods, Paul Pitchford, North Atlantic Books, California, 1993

The New Raw Energy, Leslie and Susannah Kenton, Vermilion, London, 1994

Lean Revolution, Leslie Kenton, Ebury Press, London, 1994

Juice High, Leslie Kenton with Russell Cronin, Ebury Press, London, 1996

Raw Energy Food Combining Diet, Leslie Kenton, Ebury Press, London 1996

HYDROTHERAPY

Water and Nature Cure, C Leslie Thomson, King's Clinic, Edinburgh, 1955

Uses of Water, J H Kellogg MD, The Office of The Health Reformer, 1876

Practical Hydrotherapy, Gerard Leibold, Thorsons, 1980

Hydrotherapy, Clarence Dail MD and Charles Thomas PhD, Teach Services, Bushton, New York, 1989

Manual of Hydrotherapy and Massage, Fred B Moor, Stella C Paterson, Ethel M Manwell, Mary C Nobel, Gertrude Muench, Pacific Press Publishing Association, Boise, Idaho, 1964

The Complete Water Therapy, Dian Dincin Buchman, Keats Publishing Inc., New Canaan, Connecticut, 1994

FELDENKRAIS

Mindful Spontaneity, Ruthy Alon, Prism Press, 1990

Body and Mature Behaviour: A Study of Anxiety, Sex, Gravitation and Learning, Moshe Feldenkrais, International Universities Press, New York, 1950

Awareness Through Movement: Health Exercises for Personal Growth, Moshe Feldenkrais, Harper & Row, New York/London, 1972

The Elusive Obvious, Moshe Feldenkrais, Meta Publications, Cupertino, CA., 1981

The Master Moves, Moshe Feldenkrais, Meta Publications, Cupertino, CA., 1984

The Case of Nora, Moshe Feldenkrais, Harper & Row, London, 1977

The Potent Self: A Guide to Spontaneity, Moshe Feldenkrais, Harper & Row, New York/London, 1985

XENOESTROGENS

Passage to Power, Leslie Kenton, Ebury Press, London, 1995

SPIRITUAL REJUVENATION

The Hero With a Thousand Faces, Joseph Campbell, Bollingen, Princeton University Press, 1968

The Inner Reaches of Outer Space, Joseph Campbell, Harper & Row, New York, 1988

The Power of Myth, Joseph Campbell with Bill Moyers, Doubleday, New York, 1988

Index

Index